CW01065107

STUDENT UNIT GUIDE

NEW EDITION

AQA AS Economics Unit 2
The National Economy

Ray Powell

PHILIP ALLAN

Philip Allan Updates, an imprint of Hodder Education, an Hachette UK company, Market Place, Deddington, Oxfordshire OX15 0SE

Orders
Bookpoint Ltd, 130 Milton Park, Abingdon, Oxfordshire, OX14 4SB
tel: 01235 827827
fax: 01235 400401
e-mail: education@bookpoint.co.uk
Lines are open 9.00 a.m.–5.00 p.m., Monday to Saturday, with a 24-hour message answering service.
You can also order through the Philip Allan Updates website: www.philipallan.co.uk

© Ray Powell 2011

ISBN 978-1-4441-4827-5

First printed 2011
Impression number 5 4
Year 2015 2014 2013

All rights reserved; no part of this publication may be reproduced, stored in a retrieval system, or transmitted, in any form or by any means, electronic, mechanical, photocopying, recording or otherwise without either the prior written permission of Philip Allan Updates or a licence permitting restricted copying in the United Kingdom issued by the Copyright Licensing Agency Ltd, Saffron House, 6–10 Kirby Street, London EC1N 8TS.

Printed in Dubai

Hachette UK's policy is to use papers that are natural, renewable and recyclable products and made from wood grown in sustainable forests. The logging and manufacturing processes are expected to conform to the environmental regulations of the country of origin.

P01928

Contents

Getting the most from this book

Examiner tips

Advice from the examiner on key points in the text to help you learn and recall unit content, avoid pitfalls, and polish your exam technique in order to boost your grade.

Knowledge check

Rapid-fire questions throughout the Content Guidance section to check your understanding.

Knowledge check answers

1 Turn to the back of the book for the Knowledge check answers.

Summary

Summaries

● Each core topic is rounded off by a bullet-list summary for quick-check reference of what you need to know.

Questions & Answers

Exam-style questions

Examiner comments on the questions
Tips on what you need to do to gain full marks, indicated by the icon **e**.

Sample student answers
Practise the questions, then look at the student answers that follow each set of questions.

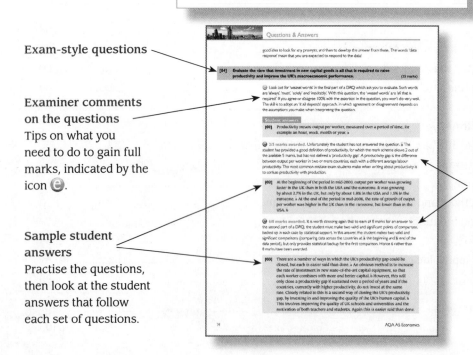

Examiner commentary on sample student answers
Find out how many marks each answer would be awarded in the exam and then read the examiner comments (preceded by the icon **e**) following each student answer. Annotations that link back to points made in the student answers show exactly how and where marks are gained or lost.

About this book

The aim of this Guide is to prepare students for the AQA Advanced Subsidiary ECON 2 examination assessing **Unit 2: The National Economy**.

Content Guidance

Start off by reading the Content Guidance section of the book which divides the Unit 2 specification into ten separate topics. You can read all the topics, one by one, before proceeding to the Questions and Answers section of the Guide. Alternatively, you may decide to read a particular topic and then to read the part of the Questions and Answers section that relates to the topic. The topics more or less follow the order of the Unit 2 specification, proceeding from National income, economic growth and the economic cycle and then on to Evaluating national economic performance.

Questions and Answers

You should read the Questions and Answers section of the book after reading all ten specification topics in the Content Guidance section, or bit by bit, having revised a selected topic covering a particular part of the specification.

Objective-test questions (OTQs)

There are ten objective-test questions (OTQs) and six data-response questions (DRQs) in the Questions and Answers section of the Guide. The OTQs are questions typical of those commonly set on each of the ten topics in the Content Guidance section of the Guide. Each of these questions is similar in layout, structure and style to an OTQ in the ECON 2 examination paper. A commentary has been included after each question to explain the correct answer and any other important features.

Data-response questions (DRQs)

You can use the six data-response questions (DRQs) either as timed test questions in the lead-up to the examination or to reinforce your understanding of the specification subject matter, topic by topic, as you proceed through the Content Guidance. In this Guide, the data-response questions are numbered 1 to 6, but in the AQA exam you will eventually sit, the two questions will be numbered **Context 1** and **Context 2**.

This section covering the data-response questions also includes:
- A student's answer for each DRQ.
- Examiner's comments on each student's answer explaining, where relevant, how the answer could be improved. These comments are denoted by the icon ⓔ.

Using other economics resources

This Guide should be used as a supplement to other resources, such as class notes, textbooks, *Economic Review* magazine and *AS/A-Level Economics Exam Revision Notes*. (The last two of these are published by Philip Allan Updates.) As this Guide contains

summaries rather than in-depth coverage of all the topics in the specification, you should not use the Guide as your sole learning resource during the main part of the course. However, you may well decide to use the Guide as the key resource in your revision programme. You are strongly advised to make full use of the Questions and Answers section, especially in the revision period when you should be concentrating on improving your examination skills.

Content guidance

Summary of the specification

The AQA specification for The National Economy contains the following sections.

3.2.1 The measurement of macroeconomic performance

Although the measurement of macroeconomic performance is the first in the list of topics in The National Economy specification, in this Guide much of the topic is covered in the last rather than the first section of the Content Guidance part of the book. (The exception is the part of the topic covering the economic cycle, which features in the section that follows this introduction.)

The specification states that students should be familiar with the data which are commonly used to measure the performance of an economy, such as gross domestic product (GDP) data, and different ways in which unemployment and inflation are measured. These and other data are often used as **economic indicators**. An economic indicator provides information on how well or how badly the economy is performing, in terms of achieving desired targets or goals, such as economic growth and higher living standards, full employment and control of inflation.

These and other targets, such as a satisfactory balance of payments, form the **policy objectives** that governments wish to achieve. It is generally best to explain how *policy indicators* are used to measure and assess macroeconomic performance after surveying the different *policy objectives*, and also the **policy instruments**, such as monetary and fiscal policy, that are used to try to achieve the objectives.

An economic indicator provides information on whether a particular aspect of macroeconomic policy is on course to achieve its objective. For example, data on the money supply are used to indicate the tightness or looseness of **monetary policy**. Too fast a rate of growth of the money supply might indicate that the main **monetary policy instrument** (the **rate of interest**) should be raised to enable the **monetary policy objective** (**control of inflation**) to be achieved.

Economic indicators are also used to compare the economic performance of the UK economy (or indeed any economy) with that of other countries. Occasionally, a data-response question in the examination may include data for four or five countries on performance indicators such as comparative economic growth rates, employment and unemployment statistics, inflation rates and trade balances.

3.2.2 How the macroeconomy works: *AD/AS* analysis, the circular flow of income, and related concepts

This is the theoretical core of the specification, focusing on two inter-related macroeconomic models of the economy: the **aggregate demand/aggregate supply (*AD/AS*) model** and the **circular flow model**.

Aggregate demand in the economy is defined as the total planned spending on real national output of all the economic agents in the economy. Aggregate demand is the sum of total planned consumption spending by households, total planned investment spending by firms, government spending and the net amount spent on the economy's output by the rest of the world (spending on exports minus spending by UK residents on imports – or net export demand).

In much the same way, **aggregate supply** represents the total output of real goods and services which all the firms or producers in the economy plan to supply or sell. The availability and quality of factors of production (e.g. capital, labour and the state of technology) determine aggregate supply. Aggregate supply is also determined by the impact of institutional and cultural factors, such as the existence of an entrepreneurial culture and appropriate incentives for taking risks and supplying labour. An important distinction is made between **short-run aggregate supply (SRAS)** and **long-run aggregate supply (LRAS)**. Long-run aggregate supply, which is determined by the economy's ability to produce, is the level of output the economy produces when on its production possibility frontier.

AD curves and *AS* curves are brought together in the aggregate demand/aggregate supply (*AD/AS*) model of the macroeconomy. **Macroeconomic equilibrium** occurs at the level of real national income or output at which total planned spending equals the quantity of goods and services firms are willing and able to supply, i.e. at the level of output at which $AD = AS$.

The circular flow model of the macroeconomy, which maps the flows of income, output and spending around the economy, also shows macroeconomic equilibrium. In this model, macroeconomic equilibrium occurs when planned injections of spending into the flow of income and spending circulating round the economy exactly equal planned withdrawals or leakages of spending out of the flow.

3.2.3 Economic performance

The performance of the national economy can be measured by the extent to which the government's **macroeconomic policy objectives** have been achieved and by the extent to which these objectives can continue to be achieved in future years.

Policy objectives are targets that the government wishes to achieve. At all times you should remember that the ultimate purpose of government policy is to improve economic welfare, which you can think of as human happiness. More narrowly, the specification requires knowledge and understanding of four objectives of government macroeconomic policy. These are:

- **full employment** (or low unemployment)

- **economic growth** (and higher living standards)
- **control of inflation**
- **a satisfactory balance of payments**

Unlike the first three objectives, which are **internal policy objectives** relating to the domestic economy, the fourth is an **external objective** that involves the UK's relations with the rest of the world. In recent years, the external objective has tended to be stated in terms of achieving or supporting a particular exchange rate rather than in terms of the balance of payments. (In this Guide, reference is also made to a fifth policy objective: a fair or equitable distribution of income and wealth.)

If all five objectives could be achieved simultaneously all the time, the economic problem would largely disappear. However, it is very difficult and perhaps impossible to achieve this. Very often, the more successful a government is at hitting one particular objective, the poorer is its performance with regard to one or more of the other objectives. Governments are often faced with **policy conflicts**, which they may try to resolve by trading off between competing objectives. (A **trade-off** occurs when a government tries to achieve an acceptable level of performance with regard to two competing objectives, because it is difficult and perhaps impossible to achieve both fully at the same time. For example, the government might aim for a 3.0% unemployment rate and a 2.0% inflation rate, because it believes that absolute full employment and zero inflation are mutually exclusive and impossible to achieve together.)

3.2.4 Macroeconomic policy

Whereas specification section 3.2.3 covers the objectives of macroeconomic policy, this section is concerned with the types of economic policy, or **policy instruments**, used to try to achieve the objectives. This involves **fiscal policy**, **monetary policy** and **supply-side policies**.

Fiscal policy covers **taxation** and **government spending** and the **government's budget deficit or surplus**, while **interest rates** are the main monetary policy instrument. In the past, fiscal policy was mostly used to influence aggregate demand. Between 2008 and 2010, fiscal policy was again used in this way. This was known as the **fiscal stimulus**, which was an attempt to 'spend the UK economy' out of **recession**. The fiscal stimulus ended in 2010 and has been replaced by **fiscal austerity** in which government spending has been cut and taxation increased to reduce the size of the budget deficit. Currently, fiscal policy is also aimed more at the supply side of the economy than at the demand side, and at maintaining macroeconomic stability.

Monetary policy involves raising or lowering interest rates primarily to manage aggregate demand in pursuit of the objective of controlling inflation. The specification also requires you to understand how monetary policy may affect the money supply and the exchange rate, and the role of the Bank of England in implementing monetary policy. One way of increasing the money supply is **quantitative easing (QE)**. ECON 2 exam questions will *not* mention quantitative easing but basic knowledge of QE can lend depth and breadth to exam answers on monetary policy.

It is now generally agreed that the success of the UK economy depends on how well the supply side of the economy performs. Consequently, much emphasis is now placed

on supply-side policies. Supply-side policies are free-market and anti-interventionist and increase the economy's production potential by improving competition and the efficiency of markets and resource allocation.

Finally, you must use the *AD/AS* macroeconomic model (part of the core of The National Economy specification, explained in section 3.2.2) to illustrate, analyse and evaluate the effects of monetary, fiscal and supply-side policies. Because monetary policy is used to influence aggregate demand in the national economy, its main effect is to shift the *AD* curve to the right or to the left. (In the long run, however, successful monetary policy also shifts the long-run aggregate supply (*LRAS*) curve to the right by achieving low and stable inflation.) For the most part, supply-side policies, which include supply-side fiscal policy, are used to shift the *LRAS* curve to the right. (As noted, fiscal policy *can* be used as a *demand-side policy* to manage aggregate demand and shift the *AD* curve to the left or right.)

National income, economic growth and the economic cycle

These notes relate to AQA specification sections 3.2.3 and 3.2.1 and prepare you to answer AQA examination questions on:
- national income
- economic growth
- the economic cycle

Essential information

National income

You must always remember that the main purpose of economic activity is to improve economic welfare and people's standards of living. For the most part, this requires increased levels of consumption of material goods and services, which in turn requires the economy to produce higher levels of output or national income.

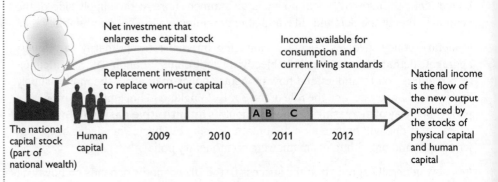

Figure 1 The production of national income

To understand national income, you must appreciate the difference between stocks and flows. There is always a **national capital stock** (the stock of natural resources and capital goods accumulated from previous production) and a **stock of human capital** (the skills of the working population). These are depicted by the symbols in the left-hand part of Figure 1. National income (shown by the large arrow in Figure 1) is the flow of new output produced in a particular period (for example, 2011) by combining the economy's stocks of physical and human capital.

This flow of new output can be measured in three ways. When measured as the output produced by the economy, it is often called **national product**. It can also be called **national income** when measured by the incomes paid to the owners of the capital and labour (and other factors of production) that produce the output. Finally, it can be called **national expenditure** when measured by the expenditure of these incomes upon the output. Since these are simply three different ways of measuring the same flow of new output, it follows that:

national output (or national product) = national income = national expenditure

You must appreciate that national income, national output and national product have exactly the same meaning, namely the flow of new goods and services produced by an economy in a particular time period, e.g. a year. However, you must understand the difference between the *real* and the *nominal* values of each of the terms. **Real national income** (output or product) refers to the actual goods and services produced by the economy, measured in physical units such as the quantity of cars or financial services produced. By contrast, **nominal national income** (output or product) measures the flow of new goods and services in monetary terms, namely at the price level when the output was produced. (Nominal national income is also called money national income.)

The relationship between nominal national income and real national income is:

nominal national income = real national income × the price level

The large arrow in Figure 1 shows the flow of national income over 4 years: 2009, 2010, 2011 and 2012. When producing national income in a particular year (2011, for example), part of the national capital stock wears out. Unless worn-out capital is replaced, the national capital stock shrinks and negative economic growth occurs. To prevent this, part of 2011's national income (shown by rectangle A in Figure 1) must be invested to repair or make good the size of the capital stock. **Gross national product (GNP)** refers to national income before deducting the amount of income invested to maintain the capital stock. **Net national product (NNP)** measures national income or output after this payment has been made. Although the specification does not require knowledge of this distinction, GNP data may appear in examination questions, as may another national income term, **gross domestic product (GDP)**. GDP is similar to GNP, but measures the flow of output produced within the UK. By contrast, GNP includes profits flowing to UK companies from their activities overseas, while deducting profits flowing out of the UK made by overseas multinational companies. Like national income and national output, GDP can also be measured in terms of either real GDP or nominal GDP.

Stocks These accumulate over time (such as wealth) and are measured at a particular point.

Flow This is continuous (such as the flow of income) and can be measured only per period of time, e.g. weekly, monthly or yearly.

Knowledge check 1

What is the difference between a capital good and human capital?

Examiner tip

The Unit 2 specification does not require you to know the difference between nominal (or money) national income and real national income, but it is useful to understand the distinction.

Knowledge check 2

Distinguish between gross investment and net investment.

Real GDP This is the flow of actual goods and services produced domestically within an economy in a particular time period, before making deduction for the wear and tear of the capital goods which produce the flow of new goods and services.

Nominal GDP (or money GDP) This is the same flow measured at the average price level for the period in question.

Economic growth

Economic growth is defined as the increase in the potential level of *real* output the economy can produce over a period of time, such as a year. Strictly, this is *long-run* economic growth, which is not the same as *short-run* economic growth. Long-run and short-run economic growth are illustrated in Figure 2. If initially the economy's production possibility frontier is *PPF*₁, short-run economic growth is shown by the movement from point *C* inside the frontier to point *A* on the frontier. Long-run economic growth is shown by the outward movement of the frontier to *PPF*₂. The movement from point *A* to point *B* depicts long-run economic growth. Short-run growth makes use of spare capacity and takes up the slack in the economy, whereas long-run growth increases total productive capacity.

Economic growth generally requires the stock of physical capital (or capital goods) to grow in size and for its quality to improve. The causes of economic growth include investment in both physical capital, such as plant and machinery, and human capital, such as better educated and more adaptable workers, technical progress, and growth of the working population. **Net investment** enlarges the stocks of physical and human capital, while **technical progress** leads to better-quality capital replacing capital goods that have become obsolete or out of date. Besides increasing capital productivity, these also lead to higher labour productivity, which is another feature of economic growth.

Examiner tip

Productivity is one of the most important concepts you need to know, for Unit 1 and for Unit 2. It is especially important for understanding supply-side economics (see pages 46–49).

Capital productivity
Output per unit of capital.

Labour productivity
Output per worker.

Knowledge check 3

Which diagrams are appropriate for illustrating long-run economic growth?

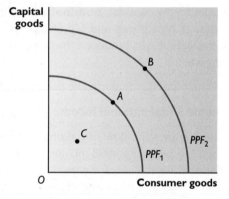

Figure 2 Economic growth illustrated by an outward movement of the economy's production possibility frontier

Actual growth and the economic cycle

As well as distinguishing between long-run and short-run economic growth, it is important to understand the difference between long-run or trend growth and actual growth.

Long-run or trend growth is shown by the rise from year to year in the smooth trend output line in Figure 3. However, the economy seldom grows smoothly in this way. Instead, the rate of economic growth fluctuates from year to year, as depicted by changes in the wavy line in the diagram. The wavy line, which shows changes in

Trend growth The average rate of economic growth over the period of at least one complete economic cycle, i.e. when the ups and downs of the cycle have been smoothed out.

actual output from year to year, illustrates the different phases of the **economic cycle**. Actual growth, which is simply the growth rate measured over the course of a particular 12-month period, may be negative as well as positive. In the UK, a recession, such as the one that began in 2008, occurs if real GDP falls for a period of 6 months or more. The recession ends in the trough of the economic cycle, which is followed by a recovery period and then possibly a boom.

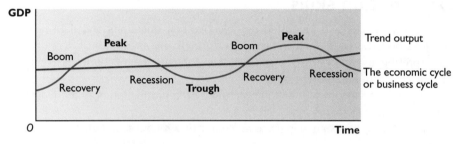

Figure 3 Trend and actual output and the economic cycle

> **Trend output** The level of output produced when the economy grows at its trend growth rate.

However, in the context of the performance of the UK economy since 1992, Figure 3 is somewhat misleading. Over the 16-year period from 1992 to 2008, the UK enjoyed continuous economic growth and there were no recessions. (However, a severe recession began in 2008 and continued through most of 2009.) In the downturn of recent economic cycles before 2008, economic growth *slowed down*, but remained *positive*. During this period, and because negative economic growth did not occur, the UK government decided to mark the beginning and end of modern economic cycles by using the concept of an output gap. An **output gap** is defined as the difference between the actual level of real output at a particular point in time and the level of output the economy would be producing had it grown continuously along the trend output line shown in Figure 4 (and also in Figure 3).

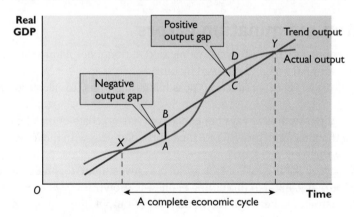

Figure 4 Output gaps and the economic cycle

A complete economic cycle is now defined as the period between two dates when the economy is judged to be on-trend, when the output gap is zero. A full economic cycle includes both a period in which output is below trend (with a negative output gap),

> **Knowledge check 4**
> What other names are used for the economic cycle?

and a period in which it is above trend (with a positive output gap). A negative output gap, shown by the distance from A to B in Figure 4, occurs when actual output is below the trend output line. By contrast, a positive output gap, shown by the distance from C to D, occurs when actual output is above the trend output line. In Figure 4, points X and Y mark the beginning and end of a complete economic cycle.

Examination skills

The skills most likely to be tested by objective-test questions and data-response questions on national income and economic growth are as follows:

- Interpreting and analysing GNP or GDP tables for a number of countries to compare levels of output and growth rates.
- Defining economic growth and illustrating it on a production possibility diagram, such as Figure 2.
- Distinguishing between a particular year's growth rate and the trend rate of growth.
- Relating the level of national income and economic growth to the economic cycle.
- Using the concept of an output gap to measure the beginning and end of an economic cycle.
- Explaining conflicts between economic growth and other objectives of government macroeconomic policy.

Examination questions

You should expect up to three objective-test questions on the terms and concepts listed in specification sections 3.2.3 and 3.2.1 on this topic. OTQ 1 in the Questions and Answers section of this Guide is a typical example. DRQ 1 covers the relationship between negative economic growth and recession, while DRQ 2 tests understanding of the links between productivity, growth and macroeconomic performance.

Common examination errors

- Failure to appreciate that national income and national output are the same.
- Confusing nominal and real national income.
- Inaccurate drawing of production possibility diagrams to illustrate economic growth.
- Asserting that growth is always beneficial and has no costs or disadvantages.
- Confusing the measured growth rate for a particular year with the underlying trend rate of growth.
- Failure to appreciate the role of factors such as investment, technical progress and quality of human capital in promoting economic growth.
- Failure to distinguish between the trend level of output, the actual level of output and the economic cycle.
- Poor understanding of output gaps and their significance for the economic cycle.

Summary

- The main purpose of economic activity is to improve economic welfare and standards of living.

- National income is the flow of new output produced in a particular period. It is also called national product.

- Gross domestic product (GDP), defined as the flow or new output produced within the economy, is the main measure used to show how much the economy is producing.

- Long-run economic growth is defined as the increase in the potential level of real output the economy can produce over a period of time, such as a year.

- Short-run economic growth, or economic recovery, occurs when the economy makes use of spare capacity, moving from a point inside the economy's production possibility frontier to a point closer to or on the frontier.

- Labour productivity is output per worker.

- Trend growth is the average rate of growth over one or more economic cycles.

- An economic cycle shows the fluctuations in actual output and growth around trend output and trend growth.

- An output gap is shown by the difference between actual output and trend output.

- A positive output gap means that actual output is above trend output.

- A negative output gap means that actual output is below trend output.

Aggregate demand and the circular flow of income

These notes relate to AQA specification section 3.2.2 and prepare you to answer AQA examination questions on:
- aggregate demand
- the determinants of consumption, saving and investment
- the accelerator and the multiplier
- the circular flow of income

Essential information

The meaning of aggregate demand

Aggregate demand comprises total *planned* spending on the real output (goods and services) that the economy produces.

Aggregate demand is represented by the following equation which you must make sure you learn and understand:

aggregate demand = consumption + investment + government spending + net exports (exports – imports)

or: $AD = C + I + G + (X - M)$

where C, I, G, X and M are the symbols used respectively for **consumption**, **investment**, **government spending** and **net export demand**, i.e. exports minus imports.

Aggregate demand
The total spending on real national output that all the economic agents in the economy wish to undertake.

Examiner tip
Don't confuse aggregate demand with aggregate supply, which is explained in the next section of this Guide (pp. 20–25).

The components of aggregate demand

Consumption, **investment**, **government spending** and **net export demand** are known as the components of aggregate demand. If the value of any of these components changes, aggregate demand also changes, either increasing or decreasing.

Each of the components of aggregate demand originates in a different sector of the economy. Households are responsible for consumption, and firms for investment, while government spending and net export demand $(X - M)$ originate respectively in the government sector and the overseas sector.

Consumption

The factors that determine household consumption in the economy also determine household saving. When consumption rises, saving falls, and vice versa. The determinants of consumption (and saving) include:

Interest rates. The rate of interest rewards savers for sacrificing current consumption, and the higher the rate of interest, the greater is the reward. Thus at any particular level of income, the amount saved increases as the real rate of interest rises and the amount spent on consumption falls.

The level of income. Consumption rises as income increases, but it generally rises at a slower rate than income. As a result, households save more as their incomes increase. The famous economist John Maynard Keynes, who more or less invented modern macroeconomics, believed that the level of income is the most important determinant of consumption and saving.

Expected future income. The current level of income in a particular year may have much less influence upon a person's planned consumption than some notion of expected income over a much longer time period, perhaps extending over the individual's remaining life. Many people save, especially early in their working lives, to finance house purchase, and then continue to save to finance retirement or to protect dependants against the financial problems that would result from the saver's early death. Saving undertaken over a number of years is followed in later years by dissaving when a house is purchased or upon retirement.

Wealth. When household wealth increases — for example, when house prices or share prices rise — people often decide to consume more and save less. For members of households, an increase in wealth does their saving for them.

Consumer confidence. When consumer confidence increases, households generally spend more and save less, whereas a fall in optimism (or a growth in pessimism) has the opposite effect. This links in with the wealth effect just described. As well as becoming wealthier, owner-occupiers become more confident about the future when house prices are rising faster than general inflation. Rapidly rising house prices lead to a consumer spending spree in the shops.

The availability of credit. When credit becomes easy to obtain, consumption increases as people supplement current income by borrowing on credit created by the banking system.

Examiner tip
Consumption, which is spending by households on domestically produced output, does *not* include spending on imports. Imports take demand out of the economy, whereas consumption is the main component of aggregate demand.

Macroeconomics The part of economics that looks at the economy in *aggregate*, for example the aggregate level of real output and its rate of growth, and the aggregate level of unemployment.

Knowledge check 5
Distinguish between consumption, saving and investment.

Investment

Investment must not be confused with saving. As a general rule, households save while firms invest. Investment is defined as total planned spending by firms on capital goods, such as plant, machinery and raw materials. The determinants of investment include:

The rate of interest. From a firm's point of view, the rate of interest is the cost of borrowing. Firms invest more as the rate of interest falls, since it becomes cheaper to raise the funds to finance investment in new capital goods.

Business confidence. Investment increases as business confidence grows because entrepreneurs believe that higher profits can be made in the future.

Technical progress. Existing machinery will eventually become obsolete or out-of-date. Firms invest in new state-of-the-art plant and machinery, which replaces old capital equipment.

The relative prices of capital and labour. When wages rise relative to the price of capital, firms tend to adopt more **capital-intensive technologies**, replacing labour with capital.

The accelerator. A firm producing at full capacity has to invest in extra capacity in order to meet higher future demand for its output. The accelerator is the number that links the change in current output to the extra capital needed to produce the additional output. For example, if the value of the accelerator is 4, one unit of extra output *next* year requires investment in four units of extra capital *this* year.

The government sector

The government sector is a source of aggregate demand in the economy (**government spending**) and — through **taxation** — the government is also responsible for a major leakage of spending out of the circular flow of income. The net effect of government spending on aggregate demand depends on the nature of the government's budget. There are three possibilities:

- A **budget deficit ($G > T$)**, when government spending is greater than tax revenue, represents expansionary fiscal policy with the government injecting spending and demand into the economy.
- A **budget surplus ($G < T$)** is the opposite. There is a net leakage of spending out of the economy as tax revenue exceeds government spending. Fiscal policy is contractionary or deflationary.
- The government may **balance its budget** (so that $G = T$), which has a generally neutral effect on aggregate demand.

The overseas sector

Spending on UK exports by residents of other countries is an injection of spending into the UK economy and increases aggregate demand. This is shown by the symbol X. Conversely, spending by UK residents on imports produced in other countries is a leakage of spending, which decreases aggregate demand. Imports are shown by the symbol M. When $X > M$, the balance of payments on current account is generally in surplus. But when $X < M$, the current account is generally in deficit, so there is a balance of payments deficit.

Knowledge check 6

How does the rate of interest affect saving and investment?

Examiner tip

Don't confuse a budget deficit with a balance of payments deficit.

Knowledge check 7

State the different ways in which a budget deficit and a balance of payments deficit affect aggregate demand.

Balance of payments deficit Occurs when exports are less than imports, expressed as when $X < M$.

The circular flow of income

A **circular flow model**, as illustrated in Figure 5, can be used to analyse the effects of injections and withdrawals of spending on the national economy. The dashed flow lines in the diagram show the **real flows** occurring in the economy between households and firms. Households supply labour and other factor services in exchange for goods and services produced by the firms. But these *real* flows generate *money* flows of income and spending shown by the solid flow lines.

The solid flow line extending from firms to households along the left-hand side of the diagram shows income that households receive in the form of money from firms for supplying factor services. Most, but not all, of this money income is spent by households on the consumer goods and services produced by the firms. This is shown by the solid flow line labelled 'consumption' on the right-hand side of the diagram. But part of household income leaks out of the circular flow along the horizontal arrow at the top of the diagram. **Leakages** or **withdrawals** from the circular flow of income are **saving**, **taxation** and **imports** (S, T and M).

Examiner tip

Make sure you do not confuse saving with investment. Saving is a leakage from the circular flow of income, whereas investment is an injection into the flow.

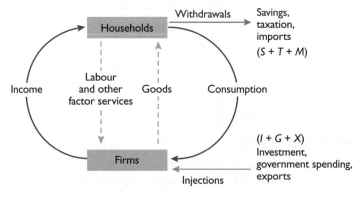

Figure 5 The circular flow of income

As well as the three leakages of saving, taxation and imports, there are three **injections** of spending into the circular flow. These are **investment**, **government spending** and **exports** (I, G and X). The three injections of demand are shown by the horizontal arrow at the bottom of the diagram.

A first look at macroeconomic equilibrium

If the three leakages of spending out of the circular flow of income exactly equal the three injections (i.e. if $S + T + M = I + G + X$), the economy is in a state of **macroeconomic equilibrium**. Conversely, if leakages exceed injections or vice versa, there is macroeconomic disequilibrium.

The multiplier

The **national income multiplier** measures the relationship between an initial change in a component of aggregate demand, such as government spending, and the resulting change in the level of national income. Suppose, for example, that government spending increases by £10 billion and that households receive this sum. Most, but not all, of the £10 billion is then spent on consumption — though part of it leaks into saving, taxation and imports. The fraction spent on consumption

AQA AS Economics

increases shopkeepers' incomes. At the next stage, the shopkeepers spend a fraction of their extra income on consumption, which causes a further increase in consumer demand. The process continues with successive spending increases, each of which is accompanied by an equal increase in national income and output.

Because the total amount by which income and output increases is a multiple of the initial increase in spending, the process is known as the **multiplier process**. For example, if the size of the multiplier is 5, an initial increase in government spending of £10 billion causes national income to rise by £50 billion. To capture the flavour of the multiplier process, think of ripples spreading over a pond after throwing a stone into the water. Each of the ripples resembles a stage in the multiplier process.

Comparing the multiplier and the accelerator

The previous section explains the government spending multiplier. Another multiplier is the **investment multiplier**. Students often confuse the investment multiplier with the **accelerator**, which is mentioned in the earlier section covering the determinants of investment. The accelerator works in the opposite direction to the investment multiplier. Whereas the investment multiplier measures how a change in private sector investment induces a change in the equilibrium level of national income, which ends up as a multiple of the initial change in investment, the accelerator measures how a change in the rate of growth of national income induces a change in the level of investment. Objective-test questions often test your understanding of the multiplier and the accelerator, and the difference between the two concepts.

Examination skills

The skills most likely to be tested by objective-test and data-response questions on aggregate demand and the circular flow of income are as follows:
- Understanding the meaning of aggregate demand and the components of aggregate demand.
- Explaining two or three of the determinants of consumption (and/or saving).
- Explaining two or three of the determinants of investment.
- Interpreting a circular flow diagram in an objective-test question.
- Using a circular flow diagram to explain how a change in a component of aggregate demand may affect the economy.
- Defining the multiplier and the accelerator and explaining both processes.

Examination questions

You should expect up to three objective-test questions on the terms and concepts listed in specification section 3.2.2 on this topic. OTQ 2 in the Questions and Answers section of this Guide is a typical example. The circular flow macroeconomic model is unlikely to figure explicitly in a data-response question. By contrast, aggregate demand and its components C, I, G and $(X - M)$ will figure in many a data question, such as DRQs 3, 4, 5 and 6 in this Guide.

Common examination errors

Commonly made mistakes on aggregate demand and the circular flow of income include the following:

> **Examiner tip**
> The Unit 2 specification states that you will not be asked to calculate the value of either the multiplier or the accelerator. However, you should understand both concepts and not confuse the two.

> **Knowledge check 8**
> What is the difference between the investment multiplier and the accelerator?

- Confusing aggregate demand (a macroeconomic concept) with the demand for a particular good or service (a microeconomic concept).
- Failing to realise that the determinants of consumption are the same as the determinants of saving.
- Confusing saving with investment.
- Inability to explain the determinants of consumption or investment in sufficient depth.
- Badly drawn circular flow diagrams.
- Poor explanations of macroeconomic equilibrium.
- Confusing the multiplier with the accelerator.

Summary

- Aggregate demand is defined as total *planned* spending on the real output (goods and services) that the economy produces.
- The components of aggregate demand are summarised in the equation:

  $$AD = C + I + G + (X - M)$$

- Consumption, investment, government spending and net export demand are the components of aggregate demand.
- The factors which determine consumption also determine saving. The factors include the rate of interest, the level of income, expected future income, wealth, consumer confidence and the availability of credit.
- The rate of interest is also an important determinant of investment, along with business confidence, technical progress, the relative prices of capital and labour and the accelerator effect.
- The accelerator measures how a change in the rate of growth of national income induces a change in the level of investment.

- The government sector is the source of government spending (an injection into the circular flow of income), and taxation (a leakage or withdrawal from the flow).
- Likewise, the overseas sector is the source of spending on exports (an injection into the circular flow of income), and spending on imports (a leakage or withdrawal from the flow).
- Macroeconomic equilibrium occurs when leakages or withdrawals from the circular flow of income equal injections of spending into the flow (when $S + T + M = I + G + X$).
- The multiplier measures the relationship between an initial change in a component of aggregate demand and the resulting change in the level of national income.
- The government spending multiplier and the investment multiplier are two of the national income multipliers.
- The multiplier must not be confused with the accelerator.

The aggregate demand and aggregate supply macroeconomic model

These notes relate to AQA specification section 3.2.2 and prepare you to answer AQA examination questions on:

- *AD* and *AS* curves
- macroeconomic equilibrium

- the use of *AD/AS* diagrams for analysing and evaluating macroeconomic policy
- the difference between short-run and long-run aggregate supply

Essential information

Introducing *AD* and *AS* curves

Along with the circular flow model of the economy explained in the previous section, the **aggregate demand** and **aggregate supply** (*AD/AS*) macroeconomic model provides the theoretical core of The National Economy specification. At the heart of the *AD/AS* model are two curves, the **aggregate demand (AD) curve** and the **aggregate supply (AS) curve**, which are illustrated in Figure 6. The aggregate supply curve drawn in Figure 6 (and also in Figure 7) is a **short-run aggregate supply (SRAS) curve**, which differs from the **long-run aggregate supply (LRAS) curve** explained later in this section of this Guide.

The *AD* curve in Figure 6 slopes downward to the right, showing that aggregate demand for goods and services rises as the average price level falls.

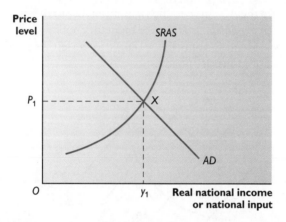

Figure 6 An *AD/AS* diagram and macroeconomic equilibrium

Just as aggregate demand comprises total spending on real national output that all the economic agents in the economy plan to undertake, so aggregate supply is the total output of goods and services which the firms or producers in the economy wish to supply and sell. In contrast to the negatively sloping *AD* curve in Figure 6, the *SRAS* curve, which slopes upward to the right, shows firms responding to higher average prices by supplying more goods and services.

Shifts of the *AD* and the *SRAS* curves

As explained in the previous section of the Guide, the position of the *AD* curve is determined by the size of the different components of aggregate demand: *C, I, G* and (*X – M*). When any of these components changes in size, the *AD* curve shifts to a new position. For example an increase in *C* shifts the *AD* curve rightward.

Costs of production is the main determinant of the position of the *SRAS* curve. For example when production costs rise, perhaps because of rising wage costs, the *SRAS* curve shifts leftward.

Aggregate demand curve Shows how much households, firms, the government and the overseas sector plan to spend on real national output at different price levels.

Aggregate supply curve Shows how much real output firms plan to produce and sell at different price levels.

Knowledge check 9
What is the difference between aggregate demand and national expenditure?

A second look at macroeconomic equilibrium

The previous section of this Guide explained how macroeconomic equilibrium occurs when leakages or withdrawals of spending from the circular flow of income equal injections of spending into the flow, i.e. when $S + T + M = I + G + X$. **Macroeconomic equilibrium** can also be defined as occurring at the level of real national income or output at which aggregate demand equals aggregate supply ($AD = AS$). In Figure 6, macroeconomic equilibrium occurs at point X, which is located above real income level y_1.

Knowledge check 10

What is the difference between macroeconomic equilibrium and micro-economic equilibrium?

Using AD/AS diagrams to analyse and evaluate macroeconomic policy

Figure 7 shows an upward-sloping SRAS curve, together with a number of AD curves. The *position* (as distinct from the *slope*) of the AD curves drawn in Figure 7 is determined by adding together all the components of aggregate demand ($C + I + G + (X - M)$). If one or more of the components of aggregate demand change, the AD curve shifts to a new position. For example, an increase in consumption, investment or export demand shifts the AD curve to the right (from AD_1 to AD_2 in Figure 7), as does a fall in imports or an *expansionary* fiscal or monetary policy. Conversely, a decrease in C, I or X, or an increase in M, shifts the AD curve to the left, as does a *contractionary* or *deflationary* fiscal or monetary policy.

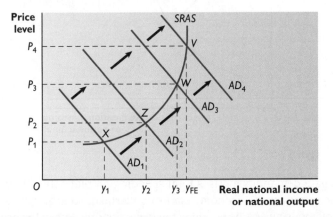

Figure 7 Using the AD/AS model to analyse the national economy

Figure 7 tells us that, with an upward-sloping SRAS curve, an increase in aggregate demand can simultaneously *reflate* real output and create jobs, and *inflate* the price level. The extent to which the demand increase is reflationary or inflationary depends on the steepness of the SRAS curve to the right of the initial macroeconomic equilibrium. Suppose, for example, that macroeconomic equilibrium is initially at point X in Figure 7, with the aggregate demand curve in position AD_1. In this situation, which depicts a recessionary economy suffering significant demand deficiency, an increase in aggregate demand to AD_2 increases both output and the price level. The increase in aggregate demand simultaneously reflates and inflates the economy, although the reflationary effect is greater as long as the SRAS curve is gently sloped. Real output and the price level both increase, to y_2 and P_2 respectively, to bring about a new macroeconomic equilibrium at point Z.

However, as the *SRAS* curve becomes steeper, any further increase in aggregate demand, for example to AD_3, is more inflationary than reflationary. The increase in aggregate demand to AD_3 moves macroeconomic equilibrium to point *W*. Real output has increased to y_3, and the price level has risen to P_3. Finally, following the move from AD_3 to AD_4, the new macroeconomic equilibrium occurs at point *V*. Real output is the **full employment level of output** (y_{FE}). The diagram tells us that any further increase in aggregate demand to the right of AD_4 solely causes inflation. The economy produces at full capacity (being on its production possibility frontier), so real output cannot increase any further, at least in the short run.

The difference between short-run and long-run aggregate supply

To recap, the upward-sloping aggregate supply curve in Figure 7 is a short-run *AS* curve, drawn under the assumption that the economy's productive capacity is fixed. However, at the full-capacity level of output y_{FE}, the economy is also producing on its long-run aggregate supply (*LRAS*) curve.

In the short run, aggregate supply depends in part upon the average price level in the economy. Firms are prepared to supply more output if the price level increases. However, in the long run, aggregate supply is not influenced by the price level. Long-run supply reflects the economy's **production potential**.

Knowledge check 11

What is the difference between inflation and deflation?

Full-employment level of output The level of real output the economy produces when everybody who wishes to work has a job. It occurs when the economy is producing on its production possibility frontier and on the *LRAS* curve.

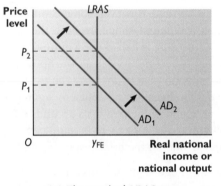

(a) The vertical *LRAS* curve

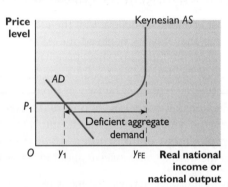

(b) The Keynesian *AS* curve

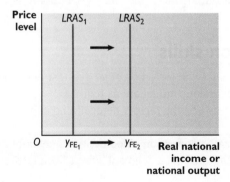

(c) Economic growth

Figure 8 *LRAS* curves

The vertical *LRAS* curve

Producing on the production possibility frontier means the labour force is fully employed. Thus, the vertical *LRAS* curve drawn in Figure 8(a) is located immediately above the full-employment level of output (y_{FE}). As the diagram shows, once the economy produces y_{FE}, an increase in aggregate demand from AD_1 to AD_2 increases average prices from P_1 to P_2, but real output remains unchanged.

Shifts of the *LRAS* curve

The vertical *LRAS* curve is located at the full-capacity and full-employment level of output. This in turn is determined by **available technology**, **productivity** (output per worker), people's motivation to work hard and/or to be **entrepreneurial**, **factor mobility**, and the effectiveness of economic **incentives** and **institutions** such as banks in providing finance to businesses.

Improvements in any of these factors increase the economy's ability to supply output and shift the *LRAS* curve to the right, as shown by the movement from $LRAS_1$ to $LRAS_2$ in Figure 8(c). A shift to the right of the *LRAS* curve illustrates economic growth, as does a similar shift of the economy's production possibility frontier. (See Figure 2 on page 12 and also the section on supply-side policies on pages 46–49.)

The Keynesian *AS* curve

Most economists believe that the *LRAS* curve is vertical. However, some economists argue that Keynes believed the *AS* curve has a different shape, in both the short run and the long run. This curve, shown in Figure 8(b), is called the **Keynesian AS curve**. The Keynesian *AS* curve is horizontal before becoming vertical. The horizontal section is explained by two of Keynes's assumptions about the way the economy functions. Keynesian economists believe that because of deficient aggregate demand, an economy can settle into a long-run equilibrium known as an **under-full employment equilibrium** (e.g. y_1 in the diagram). Because there is spare capacity, an increase in *AD* causes real output to increase, but not the price level.

However, once full employment is reached, the Keynesian *AS* curve takes on the properties of the vertical *LRAS* curve. If aggregate demand increases, only the price level and not real output increases, as the economy is already producing at full capacity.

Examination skills

The skills most likely to be tested by objective-test and data-response questions on the *AD/AS* macroeconomic model are as follows:

- Distinguishing between the factors determining aggregate demand and aggregate supply.
- Interpreting *AD/AS* diagrams in objective-test questions.
- Using *AD/AS* diagrams in a relevant way to analyse events set out in a data-response question.
- Explaining that the effects resulting from an increase in aggregate demand depend on the shape of the *AS* curve.

Knowledge check 12

What effects will a cut in the rate of income tax have on aggregate demand and aggregate supply?

Examiner tip

Be aware of the differences between demand-side (or Keynesian) and supply-side economic theory and policy.

Keynesian economics

The macroeconomic theory and policy associated with perhaps Britain's most important twentieth-century economist, John Maynard Keynes. Influential in the *fiscal stimulus* started in 2008, Keynesian economics justifies the role of government in managing aggregate demand. It is interventionist, unlike supply-side economics, which is anti-interventionist.

- Distinguishing between short-run and long-run aggregate supply (*SRAS* and *LRAS*).
- Illustrating expansionary fiscal policy and/or monetary policy using *AD/AS* diagrams.

Examination questions

You should expect up to three objective-test questions on the terms and concepts listed in specification section 3.2.2 on this topic. OTQ 3 in the Questions and Answers section of this Guide is a typical example. In data-response questions, examiners may expect you to apply the *AD/AS* macroeconomic model when answering the third and fourth parts of a data-response question. DRQs 1, 3 and 4 provide examples.

Common examination errors

Commonly made mistakes on the *AD/AS* macroeconomic model include the following:
- Confusing *AD* and *AS* curves.
- Confusing short-run and long-run aggregate supply curves (*SRAS* and *LRAS*).
- Mislabelling the axes of *AD/AS* diagrams (e.g. writing 'inflation' instead of 'price level' on the vertical axis, or 'employment' rather than 'national output' or 'real output' on the horizontal axis).
- Failure to identify the factors that can cause the *AD* curve and/or the *AS* curve to shift.
- Confusing macroeconomic *AD/AS* diagrams with microeconomic supply and demand diagrams.

> **Examiner tip**
>
> The Unit 2 specification states that students should assume that the *LRAS* curve is vertical, and have an *understanding* of the Keynesian *AS* curve. The specification implies that the Keynesian curve is both a short-run and a long-run *AS* curve.

Summary

- The *AD/AS* macroeconomic model is the main theoretical framework you are expected to use when answering data-response questions on The National Economy.
- The *AD* curve slopes downward to the right, showing that aggregate demand for real output increases the lower the price level.
- The *SRAS* curve slopes upward to the right, showing that aggregate supply of real output increases the higher the price level.
- Macroeconomic equilibrium occurs at the level of real output at which *AD* = *AS*.
- The position of the *AD* curve is determined by the size of the components of aggregate demand. If any changes in size, the *AD* curve shifts to a new position.
- The position of the *SRAS* curve is largely determined by costs of production. If costs of production change, the *SRAS* curve shifts to a new position.
- The *LRAS* curve is vertical and located at the full-employment level of real output. The economy is producing at full potential.
- The *LRAS* curve shifts to the right if potential output increases, with the economy's production possibility frontier shifting outward. A rightward shift of the *LRAS* curve shows long-run economic growth taking place.
- Improvements in technology, productivity, motivation, entrepreneurial and labour market incentives, and factor mobility can all shift the *LRAS* curve rightward, as can an improvement in the institutional set-up of the economy.

Policy objectives and conflicts

These notes relate to AQA specification section 3.2.3 and prepare you to answer AQA examination questions on:

- the objectives of government macroeconomic policy
- conflicts between policy objectives
- the trade-off between competing policy objectives

Essential information

The objectives of macroeconomic policy

In pursuit of the ultimate objective of economic policy, namely improved economic welfare for all the population, it is usual to identify five principal objectives of government macroeconomic policy. These are:

- full employment (or low unemployment)
- economic growth (and higher living standards)
- a fair or equitable distribution of income and wealth
- control of inflation (or price stability)
- an external policy objective such as a satisfactory balance of payments or a particular exchange rate target

Keynesian macroeconomic policy

The order of the list above represents a Keynesian ranking of macroeconomic policy objectives. (In the three decades following the First World War, John Maynard Keynes was the British economist most responsible for creating macroeconomic theory and policy.) Keynesian economics is generally associated with the use of demand management policies to try to achieve full employment and economic growth. To achieve these objectives, the government reflates the economy by injecting demand into the economy. In the past, both **monetary policy** and **fiscal policy** were used for this purpose, but from 1980 until recession began in 2008 only monetary policy was used. During the brief period of **fiscal stimulus** from 2008 to 2010, Keynesian fiscal policy was once again used, via tax cuts and increases in government spending, to manage aggregate demand. With a change of government, the fiscal stimulus was abandoned in 2010, giving way to **fiscal austerity**.

Expansionary or reflationary monetary policy centres mostly on cutting interest rates. However, as the economy approaches full employment, the expansion of demand tends to draw in too many imports and/or increase inflation. These problems may force the government to reverse policy in order to reduce the level of aggregate demand. Deflationary policies, such as increased interest rates (monetary policy), public spending cuts and increased taxes (fiscal policy) can be used to reduce inflationary pressures or to improve the balance of payments.

Free-market macroeconomic policy

In the early 1980s, macroeconomic policy became anti-Keynesian or pro-free market. For a number of years, an important element of pro-free market economics

Knowledge check 13

What is meant by economic growth?

Policy objective
A target or goal which policy-makers wish to achieve.

Reflationary monetary policy Fiscal or monetary policy used to increase aggregate demand, shifting the AD curve to the right.

Knowledge check 14

What is a main difference between Keynesian and pro-free market macroeconomic policy?

AQA AS Economics

was known as **monetarism**. **Monetarists** believe that inflation is caused by an excessive rate of growth of the money supply (or stock of money in the economy). They also believe that to control inflation, the rate of growth in the money supply must first be controlled.

While Keynesians generally regard full employment and economic growth as the principal policy objectives, monetarists made control of inflation the priority. Pro-free market economists and monetarists believe that competitive markets and entrepreneurship (as opposed to governments) create full employment and that governments should be **enablers** rather than **providers**. They maintain that the function of government is to foster the conditions in which competitive and efficient markets can create jobs and produce growth. One of these conditions is low inflation, which became the principal objective of free-market macroeconomic policy.

In recent years, while monetarism has become less fashionable, free-market economists have continued to support the monetarist belief that governments should actively use monetary policy to control inflation. These days, free-market macroeconomics is associated with the term **supply-side economics**, and pro-free market policies are usually supply-side policies.

Conflicts between policy objectives and trade-offs

Because of the difficulty of achieving all five macroeconomic objectives at the same time, policy-makers have often settled for the lesser goal of trading off between conflicting aims. A conflict exists when it is impossible to achieve two or more objectives at the same time. The objectives are mutually exclusive. The government attempts to resolve this conflict by achieving a relatively satisfactory performance with regard to the conflicting objectives, or it may switch periodically from one objective to another, e.g. accepting higher unemployment and lower growth (for a time) in order to reduce inflation or improve the balance of payments.

Over the years, UK macroeconomic policy has been influenced and constrained by three significant policy conflicts and policy trade-offs:

- First, there is a conflict between the **internal policy objectives** of full employment and growth and the **external objective** of achieving a satisfactory balance of payments (or possibly supporting a particular exchange rate).
- Second, there is the conflict between **full employment** and the **control of inflation**. This is often called the **Phillips curve** trade-off. (The Phillips curve is studied in Unit 4 in A2 macroeconomics.)
- Third, there is a conflict between **economic growth** and a **more equal distribution of income and wealth**. During the Keynesian era, **progressive taxation** and **transfers** to the poor were used (as part of fiscal policy) to reduce inequalities between rich and poor. In recent years, free-market supply-side economists have argued that such policies reduce entrepreneurial and personal incentives in the labour market, inhibit growth and make the economy less competitive. In the free-market view, greater inequalities may be necessary to create the labour and entrepreneurial incentives deemed necessary for rapid and sustainable economic growth.

Examiner tip

The Unit 2 specification requires you to have a good knowledge of developments in the UK economy and government policies over the 10 years before your exam. You should be able to illustrate the UK's economic cycle from the boom of the late 1980s, through the recession of the early 1990s and subsequent recovery, to the 2008 recession.

Supply-side policies
These aim to make markets function more efficiently and competitively, thereby shifting the *LRAS* curve to the right and the economy's production possibility frontier outward.

Policy trade-offs
Aiming for satisfactory performance with regard to two or more policy objectives, assuming it is impossible to achieve all the objectives simultaneously.

Knowledge check 15

What is the difference between a policy conflict and a policy trade-off?

Examiner tip
Conflicts between macroeconomic objectives have sometimes appeared to be resolved. From 1993 to 2008, UK governments were successful in achieving low unemployment, economic growth and control of inflation, though policy on improving equality and reducing the balance of payments deficit was less successful.

Examination skills

The skills most likely to be tested by objective-test and data-response questions on policy objectives and conflicts are as follows:

- Identifying and briefly explaining the meaning of the objectives of macroeconomic policy.
- Understanding the importance of different policy objectives in recent years.
- Comparing the performance of the UK and other countries in achieving policy objectives.
- Explaining how different policy instruments (monetary, fiscal and supply-side) are used to achieve particular objectives.
- Analysing policy to achieve objectives by using the *AD/AS* macroeconomic model.
- Explaining conflicts between competing policy objectives.
- Applying the concept of a trade-off to analyse and evaluate government policy.

Examination questions

You should expect up to four objective-test questions on the terms and concepts listed in specification section 3.2.3 on this topic. OTQ 4 in the Questions and Answers section of this Guide is a typical example. DRQ 3 covers the effectiveness of monetary policy in achieving the policy objective of controlling inflation, while DRQ 5 relates tax policy to supply-side policy objectives.

Common examination errors

Commonly made mistakes on policy objectives and conflicts include:

- Failure to explain the meaning of particular policy objectives, such as full employment.
- Confusing policy objectives, policy instruments, and policy and performance indicators.
- Failure to explain sufficiently particular conflicts between policy objectives.
- Failure to appreciate how the nature of policy objectives and conflicts has changed over the years.
- Inability to make relevant comparisons with other countries.

Summary

- The five principal objectives of government macroeconomic policy are full employment, economic growth, a fair distribution of income and wealth, control of inflation, and a satisfactory balance of payments.
- Keynesian macroeconomic policy centres on managing the level of aggregate demand.
- Free-market macroeconomic policy is associated with supply-side economics.

- It is difficult to achieve all five macroeconomic objectives at the same time and there are conflicts between policy objectives.
- Governments attempt to resolve the conflicts by trading off between policy objectives.
- The main trade-offs are between internal and external policy objectives, between reducing unemployment and controlling inflation, and between economic growth and greater equality.

Employment, unemployment, inflation and deflation

These notes relate to AQA specification section 3.2.3 and prepare you to answer AQA examination questions on the key macroeconomic topics of:

- full employment
- the measurement of unemployment
- types of unemployment
- inflation and deflation
- the measurement of inflation

Essential information

Full employment

Full employment occurs in the economy's aggregate labour market when the aggregate demand for labour equals the aggregate supply of labour. In Figure 9, the downward-sloping aggregate demand curve for labour shows that as the real wage rate paid to workers falls, employers or entrepreneurs are willing to employ more labour. By contrast, the aggregate supply curve of labour in Figure 9 slopes upward, showing that workers supply more labour as the real wage rate rises. Full employment occurs at E_{FE}, at the market-clearing real wage rate of W_{FE}.

> **Full employment**
> A situation in which the number of workers whom employers wish to hire equals the number of people who wish to work.

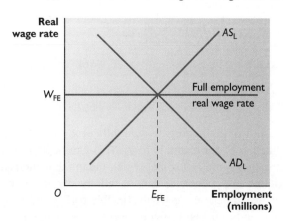

Figure 9 Full employment illustrated in the economy's aggregate labour market

> **Knowledge check 16**
> Why is a high level of employment important for an economy?

The measurement of unemployment

There is always some unemployment in the economy. The UK government measures unemployment in two ways. The best-known method is the **claimant count**, which simply measures the number of people claiming unemployment-related benefits such as the job seeker's allowance from the government. The second method of measurement is based on the **Labour Force Survey (LFS)**. The LFS is a quarterly survey of 60,000 households, which counts people as unemployed if they are actively seeking work and have not had a job during the week in question.

Types of unemployment

There are a number of different types and causes of unemployment, but some of these are studied at A2 rather than at AS. The Unit 2 specification requires that you understand cyclical, frictional, structural and seasonal unemployment.

Cyclical unemployment

Cyclical unemployment, which occurs in the downturn of the economic cycle, is also known as **demand-deficient** or **Keynesian unemployment**. The latter name reflects the fact that Keynes identified demand deficiency as an important possible cause of unemployment in the Great Depression of the 1930s. *AD/AS* and production possibility curve diagrams can both be used to illustrate cyclical unemployment. In Figure 10(a), macroeconomic equilibrium occurs at point *X*, with the level of real output y_1. However, y_1 is well below the full-employment level of output y_{FE}. The *AD* curve AD_1 is too far to the left, showing deficient aggregate demand.

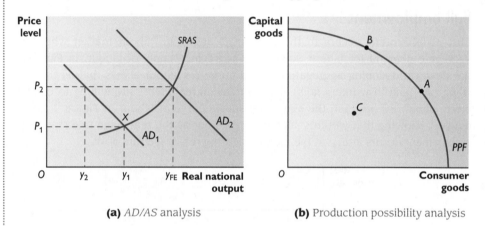

(a) *AD/AS* analysis   **(b)** Production possibility analysis

Figure 10 Using *AD/AS* and production possibility curve diagrams to illustrate cyclical unemployment

Indeed, a leftward shift of the aggregate demand curve from AD_2 to AD_1 may cause real output to fall below y_1, for example to y_2. This can happen if prices and wages in the economy are sticky and inflexible, which means that the price level remains at P_2 instead of falling to P_1. Because output falls below y_1, the recession ends up being deeper than would be the case with flexible prices and wage rates. Cyclical unemployment thus ends up being higher. Either way, whether output falls to y_1 or to y_2, aggregate demand would need to increase to AD_2 to eliminate cyclical unemployment.

Figure 10(b) shows the economy's production possibility frontier, labelled *PPF*. Full employment occurs at all points on the frontier such as *A* and *B*. However, any point inside the frontier, such as *C*, depicts a situation in which workers are unemployed because there is insufficient demand for the output they could produce.

Frictional unemployment

Change is constantly taking place in a dynamic economy, with some industries declining and others growing. As new products are developed, and demand and cost

> **Knowledge check 17**
>
> Why must there always be some unemployment in an economy?

         AQA AS Economics

conditions change, firms demand more of some labour skills while the demand for other types of labour declines. Economists use the terms frictional and structural unemployment to describe the resulting unemployment.

Frictional unemployment, as its name suggests, results from frictions in the labour market which create a delay or time-lag during which a worker is unemployed when moving from one job to another. Note that our definition of frictional unemployment assumes that a job vacancy exists and that a friction in the job market, caused by either the **geographical or occupational immobility of labour**, prevents an unemployed worker from filling the vacancy. It follows that the number of unfilled job vacancies which exist can be used as an indicator of the level of frictional unemployment in the economy.

Structural unemployment

Structural unemployment is generally more severe than frictional unemployment, resulting from the structural decline of industries which are unable to compete or adapt in the face of changing demand and new products, new techniques of producing existing products and the emergence of more efficient competitors in other countries. The **growth of international competition** and the effect of **globalisation** on the economy have contributed recently to structural unemployment. **Technological unemployment** can be regarded as a special case of structural unemployment, which results from the successful growth of new industries using labour-saving technology such as automation.

Seasonal unemployment

Seasonal unemployment, which is a form of **casual unemployment**, is a special case of frictional unemployment. Fruit pickers and workers employed in holiday resorts are often seasonally unemployed, as are building workers in very cold winters.

Policies to reduce unemployment

The appropriate policy to reduce unemployment depends on identifying correctly the underlying cause of unemployment. Expansionary monetary and/or fiscal policies are appropriate for reducing cyclical unemployment in the downturn of an economic cycle, but may fall foul of the policy conflicts described on pages 26–28. The conflict between low unemployment and controlling inflation is particularly significant. Supply-side policies rather than demand-side policies are appropriate for reducing frictional and structural unemployment.

Inflation and deflation

Inflation is defined as a persistent or continuing tendency for the price level to rise. Strictly, **deflation** is the opposite (a persistent tendency for the price level to fall), although economists often use the word to refer to the reduction in output and employment which occurs in recessions. When the government deflates the economy, it uses contractionary monetary and/or fiscal policy to reduce the level of demand and economic activity. Conversely, the government reflates the economy when it uses monetary and/or fiscal policy to expand demand.

Examiner tip
When answering a question on unemployment, decide whether it is cyclical, frictional or structural, or a mix of at least two.

Knowledge check 18
Which type of unemployment is most associated with the economist Keynes?

Knowledge check 19
Why is it important that a government correctly identifies the main cause or causes of unemployment?

Inflation A continuing rise in the average prices of all goods over an extended period of time.

Demand-pull inflation

Too much or inappropriate expansion of demand leads to inflation of the price level rather than to reflation of output and employment. For example, if unemployment is incorrectly diagnosed in terms of demand deficiency (when the true cause is structural), a policy of fiscal or monetary expansion to stimulate aggregate demand creates excess demand. Too much demand pulls up the price level, with little or no lasting beneficial effect on employment. This is called **demand-pull inflation.** The demand-pull theory of inflation is generally favoured by free-market and monetarist economists. In the **monetarist theory of demand-pull inflation**, the excess demand which pulls up the price level is blamed on an excess rate of growth of the money supply.

Cost-push inflation

By contrast, many Keynesian economists favour the **cost-push** theory of inflation. Fifty years ago, cost-push inflation was generally associated with trade unions using their monopoly power over the supply of labour to bargain for wage increases in excess of any rise in labour productivity. Keynesians argued that firms with monopoly power were prepared to pay these wage increases because they could pass on the increasing costs as price rises. At the time, trade union militancy and big business were believed to be responsible for cost-push inflation.

Imported cost-push inflation

It is now widely believed, however, that recent cost-push inflation has resulted, not from excessive wage costs, but from the rising price of imports of food, raw materials or commodities, and energy. Indeed, China has recently begun to increase the prices of the manufactured goods it exports. This is another source of imported cost-push inflation.

Inflation illustrated on AD/AS diagrams

Knowledge check 20

How does the explanation of cost-push inflation differ in the early 2000s from the explanation offered 50 years ago?

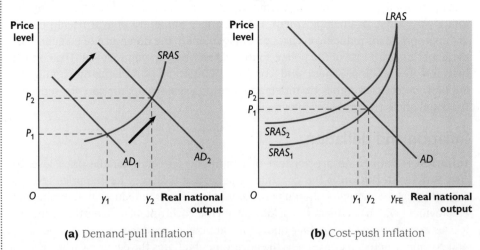

(a) Demand-pull inflation

(b) Cost-push inflation

Figure 11 Using *AD/AS* diagrams to illustrate demand-pull and cost-push inflation

The two panels of Figure 11 illustrate demand-pull and cost-push inflation. Figure 11(a) shows the average price level rising from P_1 to P_2, when the AD curve shifts to the right from AD_1 to AD_2. This is demand-pull inflation. Figure 11(b) illustrates cost-push inflation. Rising business costs, such as wages, raw material and energy costs, shift the SRAS curve upward and to the left from $SRAS_1$ to $SRAS_2$. Rising production costs push up the price level from P_1 to P_2.

The leftward shift of the SRAS curve that causes cost-push inflation also causes real output to fall from y_1 to y_2. The combination of a rising price level with falling or stagnant output is called **stagflation**.

The measurement of inflation

Until 2003, the rate of inflation was measured in the UK by changes in the retail prices index (RPI). The government still uses the RPI for this purpose, but the consumer prices index (CPI) has now become the main measure of inflation. A price index such as the RPI or CPI attempts to measure the cost of living of a representative family in the economy. Each month, the prices of all the goods in a selected 'national shopping basket' are recorded at hundreds of shops, so that the price index for that month can be calculated. Each of the items in the shopping basket is given a weight to reflect its importance in family spending. Suppose the price index this year is 105, whereas last year (the base year) it was 100. Given these numbers, a 5-point move in the index means that the rate of inflation over the year was 5%. But if the price index numbers for the two years are 110 (this year) and 105 (last year), the rate of inflation is a little below 5%. Can you work out why?

> **Price index** A number which measures the average of prices contained in a 'basket' of goods and services.

Examination skills

The skills most likely to be tested by objective-test and data-response questions on employment, unemployment, inflation and deflation are as follows:
- Explaining employment in terms of the demand for, and supply of, labour.
- Relating the growth of employment to the growth of national income and output, and the resulting job creation.
- Defining and illustrating full employment in terms of a labour market supply and demand diagram, such as Figure 9.
- Explaining cyclical, frictional, seasonal and structural unemployment.
- Understanding how unemployment is measured in the UK.
- Explaining the meaning of inflation and related terms such as deflation and reflation.
- Analysing inflation in terms of the two main theories of inflation: demand-pull and cost-push.
- Explaining and justifying appropriate policies to reduce unemployment and/or inflation.
- Understanding the policy conflict between low unemployment and low inflation.

Examination questions

You should expect up to three objective-test questions on the terms and concepts listed in specification section 3.2.3 of this topic. OTQ 5 in the Questions and Answers section of this Guide is a typical example. DRQ 4 focuses on the causes and

consequences of demand-pull and cost-push inflation, while DRQ 1 indirectly covers unemployment in the context of the economy suffering a recession.

Common examination errors

Commonly made mistakes on employment, unemployment and inflation include:
- Failing to provide an adequate definition of full employment.
- Rewriting a question so that you write all you know about the different types of unemployment, irrespective of the focus of the question.
- Failing to relate policies to reduce unemployment to causes of unemployment.
- Confusing demand-pull and cost-push causes of inflation.
- Confusing inflation with one-off price rises and with changes in the relative prices of goods and services.
- Failing to understand data on inflation presented in index number form.

Summary

- Full employment occurs when the aggregate demand for labour equals the aggregate supply of labour.
- Unemployment is measured in two different ways, by the claimant count and by the Labour Force Survey method.
- You are required to know about cyclical, frictional, structural and seasonal unemployment.
- Cyclical unemployment is caused by deficient aggregate demand in the economy.
- Frictional unemployment is 'between jobs' unemployment or transitional unemployment.

- Seasonal unemployment is caused by the seasonal nature of some occupations.
- Inflation is a continuing and persistent rise in the average price level.
- Demand-pull inflation results from excess aggregate demand pulling up the price level.
- Cost-push inflation results from rising business costs pushing up the price level, particularly these days the rising costs of imported raw materials and energy.
- The rate of inflation is measured in two main ways, by the consumer prices index and by the retail prices index.

The balance of payments on current account

These notes relate to AQA specification section 3.2.3 and prepare you to answer AQA examination questions on the key macroeconomic topics of:
- the meaning of the balance of payments on current account
- current account surpluses, deficits and equilibrium
- the different items in the current account
- strengths and weaknesses in the UK current account

Essential information

The meaning of the balance of payments on current account

The balance of payments accounts are the official record published by the government of all the currency flows into and out of the country. There are two main parts to the balance of payments: the **current account** and **capital flows**. The current account, which includes exports and imports, is so called because it measures income generated in the year in question flowing into and out of the economy.

By contrast, capital flows occur when residents of one country acquire capital assets, such as factories and oil refineries, located in other countries. Capital flows are an A2 topic, so they are not explained in these notes. Nevertheless, it is worth knowing that the acquisition of overseas-located assets leads to investment income (a current account item) flowing into the country in future years, and that capital flows affect monetary policy.

Current account surpluses, deficits and equilibrium

Very often when dealing with the current account of the balance of payments, economists simplify and pretend that there are only two items in the current account: **exports** and **imports** of goods and services (X and M). There are then three possibilities:

- When the value of exports exceeds the value of imports (i.e. when $X > M$), there is a current account **surplus**.
- When the value of exports is less than the value of imports (i.e. when $X < M$), there is a current account **deficit**.
- And finally, when the value of exports equals the value of imports (i.e. when $X = M$), there is a state of current account equilibrium. (Note that the current account is in disequilibrium when there is a surplus or a deficit.)

The different items in the current account of the balance of payments

Exports and imports

Exports and imports, which are the two main items in the current account, can be divided into **exports and imports of goods** (which make up the balance of trade in goods), and **exports and imports of services** (which form the balance of trade in services).

Investment income

The two other items in the current account which you need to understand are **net investment income** (which has already been mentioned) and **net transfers**. These are both non-trade items in the current account. Net investment income includes profits flowing to UK companies from their investments in other countries, minus net profit outflows repatriated to foreign companies from their investment in the UK. Also included are net interest payments, comprising interest received by British banks on loans they have granted overseas, minus interest payments flowing to overseas banks from their loans to clients in the UK.

Transfers

Net transfers form the second non-trade item in the current account. Examples of outward transfers from the UK are UK foreign aid and income sent overseas by immigrant workers in the UK to their families living in their countries of origin. An inward transfer would be money paid by overseas governments for the upkeep of their embassies in the UK.

Examiner tip

Make sure you don't confuse a balance of payments deficit with a budget deficit. Many students confuse the two!

Knowledge check 21

How do exports and imports affect aggregate demand?

Current account equilibrium When the money value of exports more or less equals the money value of imports over a period of time.

Balance of trade The main part of the current account comprising the balance of trade in goods and the balance of trade in services.

Examiner tip

When you answer an exam question on aggregate demand, you can represent the current account as $(X - M)$. By contrast, when answering a question on the balance of payments, remember that as well as exports and imports, investment income and transfers are also items in the current account.

Knowledge check 22

Relate investment income to capital flows.

Strengths and weaknesses in the UK current account

For most of recent history, the UK's current account has been in a substantial deficit. Although the balance of trade in services has been in surplus, this has been insufficient to offset the very large deficit in the balance of trade in goods.

The strength of the UK current account is located mostly in the export earnings of financial services and insurance. This reflects the competitiveness of the City of London in world financial markets. This strength can also be viewed as a weakness in that financial services have grown at the expense of manufacturing, reflecting 'unbalance' in the UK economy. Indeed, the UK's main weakness lies in the uncompetitiveness of UK manufactured goods in world markets. Through a process known as **deindustrialisation**, manufactured goods now account for less than 13% of UK output and most manufactured goods are now imported.

The 'credit crunch' which hit world financial markets in 2007 and 2008 had an adverse effect on the UK's financial exports and illustrated the unbalance in the UK economy. (It is worth checking whether financial export earnings have recovered in recent years.) A related weakness is in the energy sector. The UK has switched in recent years from being a net exporter of oil and gas to become a net importer in a world in which energy prices often rise and supplies can no longer be guaranteed.

The UK's large current account deficit also imposes a considerable constraint on the UK's freedom to pursue domestic economic policy. This is explained in the answer and commentary to DRQ 6.

Knowledge check 23

What is meant by a balanced economy?

Examination skills

The skills most likely to be tested by objective-test and data-response questions on the current account of the balance of payments are as follows:
- Interpreting statistics in tables or graphs showing changes in the main items in the current account.
- Understanding the meaning of current account equilibrium and deficits and surpluses.
- Relating exports and imports to aggregate demand.
- Relating exports and imports to injections and leakages of demand and the circular flow of income.
- Understanding possible conflicts between external and internal macroeconomic policy objectives.
- Analysing the effect of changes in interest rates and monetary policy (see the section on monetary policy on pages 42–45) on the current account.

Examination questions

You should expect up to four objective-test questions on the terms and concepts listed in specification section 3.2.3 on this topic. OTQ 6 in the Questions and Answers section of this Guide is a typical example. ECON 2 data-response questions often focus on the UK balance of payments. DRQ 6 tests knowledge and understanding of the UK balance of payments on current account.

Common examination errors

Commonly made mistakes on the current account of the balance of payments include:

- Confusing a current account deficit or surplus with a budget deficit or surplus.
- Assuming that UK investment overseas (a capital flow) is part of the current account.
- Failing to link exports and imports to shifts of the aggregate demand (*AD*) curve.
- Confusing the balance of trade in goods with the balance of trade in services.
- Inability to explain changes in major items in the balance of trade in goods, e.g. manufactured goods and oil and gas.
- Inability to explain changes in major items in the balance of trade in services, e.g. financial services and tourism.

- The balance of payments account attempts to measure all the currency flows into and out of the country in a particular time period.
- The ECON 2 exam tests your knowledge and understanding of the current account of the balance of payments.
- Capital flows, which form the other main part of the balance of payments, are an A2 topic and not an AS topic.
- Exports and imports of goods and services (*X* and *M*) are the main items in the current account.
- In most years, the balance of trade surplus in services is insufficient to offset the balance of trade deficit in goods, so the overall UK current account is in deficit.
- Net investment income and transfers are the other items you need to understand in the current account.
- The large surplus in the balance of trade in financial services has been the main strength in the UK current account.
- However, the financial service surplus also reflects the significant 'unbalance' in the UK economy, stemming from the decline of manufacturing industry and deindustrialisation.
- A further weakness is the increase in the deficit in the balance of trade in oil.

Summary

Fiscal policy

These notes relate to AQA specification section 3.2.4 and prepare you to answer AQA examination questions on:

- the meaning of fiscal policy
- the difference between macroeconomic and microeconomic fiscal policy
- using *AD/AS* diagrams to analyse demand-side fiscal policy
- how fiscal policy affects the pattern of economic activity

Essential information

The meaning of fiscal policy

Fiscal policy is the part of a government's economic policy aimed at achieving its economic objectives through the use of the fiscal instruments of **taxation**, **public spending** and the **budget deficit** or **surplus**.

Fiscal policy The use of government spending, taxation and the government's budgetary position to try to achieve government policy objectives.

Keynesian fiscal policy

For many years, fiscal policy was generally associated with **managing the level of aggregate demand** in order to expand (reflate) or contract (deflate) the economy. This became known as Keynesian fiscal policy and is also called **demand-side fiscal policy**. To increase aggregate demand, the government increased government spending or cut taxes. The resulting increase in the government's budget deficit injected demand into the circular flow of income. This was **expansionary fiscal policy**. By contrast, **contractionary fiscal policy** involved the opposite: cuts in government spending or tax increases which reduced the budget deficit, possibly moving the government's finances into surplus. Contractionary (or deflationary) fiscal policy took demand out of the economy.

Discretionary fiscal policy

When fiscal policy is used to raise or lower taxes and government spending in order to manage aggregate demand, it is called **discretionary fiscal policy**. Tax rates and levels of government spending are fine-tuned or regularly adjusted to try to maintain a high level of employment, while avoiding an unacceptable increase in the rate of inflation.

Free-market or supply-side fiscal policy

During recent decades, **supply-side fiscal policy** has largely replaced demand-side fiscal policy. Supply-side fiscal policy is part of a wider **supply-side policy** which aims to shift the *LRAS* curve to the right. In supply-side fiscal policy, taxes are cut, not to increase aggregate demand, but to increase incentives to work harder, to be entrepreneurial, to take risks and to invest. Under monetarist and supply-side influence, recent UK governments have believed that using fiscal policy in a demand-side way to stimulate or reflate aggregate demand to achieve growth and full employment is, in the long run, at best ineffective and at worst damaging. They argue that any growth of output and employment resulting from an expansionary fiscal policy is short-lived, and that the main effect of such a policy is inflation, which quickly destroys the conditions necessary for satisfactory market performance and wealth creation. Supply-side economics and fiscal policy have also been used to create stability in the economy, so that economic agents, particularly businesses, are not subjected to sudden surprises in the form of unexpected tax changes.

Fiscal stimulus and fiscal austerity

However, for a short period from 2008 to 2010, in response to deep recession, there was a complete U-turn in UK fiscal policy, which for a short period once again became Keynesian. Taxes were cut while government spending, the budget deficit and borrowing increased. But the Keynesian **fiscal stimulus** came to an end, partly due to a change of government, and partly because the rapid increase in government borrowing was getting out of control. The new Coalition government, dominated by the Conservatives, favoured a return to supply-side fiscal policy. Taxes were raised, government spending was severely cut, and **fiscal austerity** replaced the fiscal stimulus.

Knowledge check 24

How would you illustrate discretionary fiscal policy on an *AD/AS* diagram?

Knowledge check 25

How may supply-side fiscal policy be illustrated on an *AD/AS* diagram?

Supply-side economics
The body of economic theory and policy which favours pro-free market policies to improve the supply-side performance of the economy by making markets more efficient and competitive.

Examiner tip
Exam questions may require you to have knowledge and understanding of recent events in the UK economy.

The use of an automatic fiscal policy rule

By rejecting demand-side or Keynesian fiscal policy, supporters of supply-side fiscal policy also generally reject the use of discretionary fiscal policy. Some argue that the government should use an **automatic fiscal policy** rule always to **balance the budget**, i.e. to set G equal to T. Budget deficits and surpluses must not be allowed to occur.

The microeconomic elements of fiscal policy

Unlike monetary policy, fiscal policy is used in a microeconomic as well as in a macroeconomic way. As already noted, supply-side fiscal policy focuses on the incentives and disincentives that result respectively from low and high tax rates. On the government spending side of microeconomic fiscal policy, changes to the benefits system (particularly unemployment benefits) are made to alter the labour or leisure choice in favour of working rather than choosing voluntary unemployment.

At the macro level, fiscal policy affects the *level* of economic activity. By contrast, at the micro level fiscal policy affects the *pattern* of economic activity, for example state provision of **public goods** and **merit goods**, and the use of expenditure taxes and subsidies to alter the relative prices of goods and services. (This element of fiscal policy is part of the Unit 1 specification and is assessed by ECON 1 exam questions on market failure.)

Using AD/AS diagrams to analyse demand-side fiscal policy

As noted above, demand-side fiscal policy or Keynesian fiscal policy operates through increasing or decreasing aggregate demand. Government spending (G) is one of the components of aggregate demand. An increase in government spending or a cut in taxation increases the size of the budget deficit (or reduces the size of the budget surplus). Either way, an injection into the circular flow of income occurs and the effect on aggregate demand is expansionary.

Incentives Motivations for people to behave in particular ways, e.g. to work harder.

Disincentives Deterrents that discourage certain types of behaviour, e.g. slacking at work.

Examiner tip
For ECON 2, you only need to know about macroeconomic fiscal policy. Nevertheless, knowledge of the microeconomic nature of some elements of fiscal policy can be useful, particularly if you are sitting the ECON 1 exam in the same exam session as the ECON 2 exam.

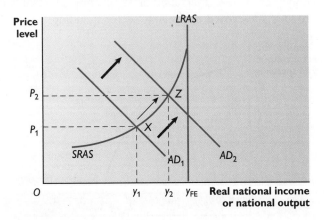

Figure 12 Keynesian or demand-side fiscal policy

Figure 12 illustrates the effect of such an expansionary or reflationary fiscal policy. Initially, with the aggregate demand curve in position AD_1, macroeconomic equilibrium occurs at point X. Real income or output is y_1, and the price level is P_1.

To eliminate the cyclical (demand-deficient or Keynesian) unemployment, the government increases the budget deficit by raising the level of government spending or by cutting taxes. The expansionary fiscal policy shifts the AD curve to the right from AD_1 to AD_2, and the economy moves to a new macroeconomic equilibrium at point Z.

As previously explained, the extent to which expansionary fiscal policy reflates real output (in this case from y_1 to y_2), or creates excess demand that leads to demand-pull inflation (in this case an increase in the price level from P_1 to P_2), depends on the shape of the AS curve, which in turn depends on how close initially the economy was to full employment. The nearer the economy gets to full employment, the greater the inflationary effect of expansionary fiscal policy and the smaller the reflationary effect.

Figure 12 can be adapted to illustrate the effect of a contractionary or deflationary fiscal policy. In this case a cut in government spending or an increase in taxation shifts the AD curve to the left.

Fiscal policy and the government spending multiplier

Government spending multiplier Measures the relationship between a change in government spending and the resulting change in the equilibrium level of nominal national income.

When used in a macroeconomic way to manage aggregate demand, an important concept is the **government spending multiplier**. For example, if the size of the government spending multiplier is 4, an initial increase in government spending of £10 billion increases nominal national income by £40 billion. Most of the extra real output is produced by the private sector rather than by the government.

Fiscal policy and possible crowding out

Knowledge check 26

Contrast the government spending and the investment multiplier. Name two other multipliers.

However, besides causing inflation rather than an increase in real output, many free-market economists believe that another significant effect of an increase in government spending is to **crowd out** private sector spending.

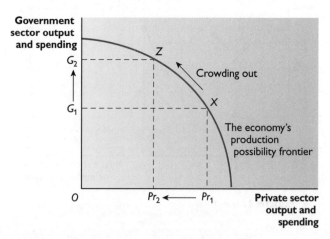

Figure 13 Government spending crowding out private sector spending

The production possibility frontier in Figure 13 illustrates crowding out. If the economy is initially at point X on its production possibility frontier, an increase in government spending from G_1 to G_2 displaces or crowds out private spending by Pr_1 minus Pr_2. The new combination of government spending and private sector spending is shown at point Z on the production possibility frontier. Government spending grows at the expense of private sector spending, but there is no overall increase in output.

How taxation affects the economy

Taxation is used to finance government spending, though when there is a budget deficit government borrowing also finances public spending. As already noted, expenditure taxes and subsidies alter economic behaviour by changing the relative prices of goods and services. Taxation also reduces the amount of income that people have available to spend on consumption or imports.

The effect of progressive taxation

Progressive taxation leads to the rich paying a larger proportion of their income on taxes than the poor. Keynesian governments transferred the revenue raised from progressive taxation to the poor, in the form of **welfare benefits**. This altered the distribution of income in favour of lower-income groups. As a result, patterns of production and spending changed away from goods and services consumed by the better-off to those consumed by the poor.

Knowledge check 27

What is the difference between progressive and regressive taxation?

Progressive taxation and incentives

Free-market economists believe that progressive taxation and transfers to the poor have a bad effect on personal incentives, reducing the incentives to work and to be entrepreneurial, while increasing the incentive to live off benefits. The supply-side fiscal policy advocated by free-market economists attempts to reduce taxation, government spending and the size of the state, thereby freeing up resources for the private sector to use.

Examination skills

The skills most likely to be tested by objective-test and data-response questions on fiscal policy are as follows:

- Defining fiscal policy and distinguishing it from monetary policy.
- Understanding links between fiscal policy and monetary policy.
- Explaining how fiscal policy can be used to manage aggregate demand and discussing the limitations of using fiscal policy in this way.
- Illustrating demand-side fiscal policy on an *AD/AS* diagram and explaining how the effectiveness of the policy depends on the nature of aggregate supply.
- Describing and explaining the main elements of supply-side fiscal policy implemented in the UK in recent years.
- Relating fiscal policy to the macroeconomic policy objectives of full employment, growth and controlling inflation.
- Applying in a relevant way fiscal policy concepts such as the budget deficit or surplus, and government or public-sector borrowing that finances a deficit.
- Explaining how fiscal policy affects the pattern of economic activity.

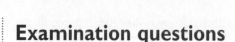

Examination questions

You should expect up to three objective-test questions on the terms and concepts listed in specification section 3.2.4 on this topic, although only one or two may focus exclusively on fiscal policy. OTQ 7 in the Questions and Answers section of this Guide is a typical example. DRQ 5 tests knowledge and understanding of the nature of UK fiscal policy.

Common examination errors

Commonly made mistakes on fiscal policy include the following:

- Confusing fiscal policy with monetary policy.
- Inability to use an *AD/AS* diagram to illustrate the impact of fiscal policy on the national economy.
- Confusing a budget deficit (or surplus) with a balance of payments deficit (or surplus).
- Inability to relate a budget deficit (or surplus) to injections into (or withdrawals from) the circular flow of income.
- Failure to understand that many aspects of recent and current fiscal policy in the UK illustrate supply-side economic policy.
- Poor understanding of concepts such as progressive taxation and transfers.

Summary

- Fiscal policy is the part of a government's economic policy aimed at achieving its economic objectives through the use of the fiscal instruments.
- Fiscal policy instruments are taxation, public spending and the budget deficit or surplus.
- Demand-side fiscal policy, or Keynesian fiscal policy, manages aggregate demand.
- Along with other supply-side policies, supply-side fiscal policy aims to shift the *LRAS* curve to the right.

- Supply-side fiscal policy tries to create incentives by cutting tax rates and making it less attractive to claim welfare benefits.
- Supply-side fiscal policy is often microeconomic rather than macroeconomic.
- Taxation is used to finance government spending, as is government borrowing.
- Progressive taxation and transfers of tax revenue to lower income groups reduce income inequality, but may also adversely affect incentives.

Monetary policy

These notes relate to AQA specification section 3.2.4 and prepare you to answer AQA examination questions on:

- the meaning of monetary policy
- the role of the Bank of England in implementing monetary policy
- the instruments and objectives of monetary policy
- using *AD/AS* diagrams to analyse monetary policy
- linking monetary policy to the exchange rate and the balance of payments

Essential information

The meaning of monetary policy

Monetary policy is any deliberate action undertaken by the government or its agents, such as the country's **central bank**, to achieve economic objectives by using monetary instruments such as the rate of interest, quantitative easing and controls over bank lending.

The role of the Bank of England in implementing monetary policy

Until 1997, UK monetary policy was implemented more or less jointly by the **Treasury** (the government's finance ministry) and the central bank, the **Bank of England**. In 1997, the Bank of England was made independent and it is now the sole monetary authority, with a duty to achieve the monetary policy target set by the Treasury.

The instruments of monetary policy

In the past, controls over bank lending and controlling the growth of the money supply were used as monetary policy instruments. These days, monetary policy operates mostly through the interest rate that the Bank of England's Monetary Policy Committee sets each month. The Bank's interest rate or lending rate is also called Bank Rate. A change in the Bank of England's interest rate quickly affects other short-term interest rates (such as the overdraft rates that banks charge to personal and business customers), and usually affects mortgage interest rates at which homeowners borrow over the long term. For a short period from March 2009 until February 2010, and in response to the collapse of aggregate demand in the recession which started in 2008, a monetary policy instrument known as **quantitative easing (QE)** supplemented interest rate policy in UK monetary policy. By increasing the money supply, quantitative easing increases aggregate demand, but it may also lead to inflation.

The objectives of monetary policy

By raising or lowering its own interest rate, Bank Rate (or indeed by leaving Bank Rate unchanged), the Bank of England hopes to influence the interest rates set by commercial banks, and thereby to manage the level of aggregate demand. This is done to try and achieve the policy objective set by the government, which is control of inflation.

Prior to May 1997, monetary policy was concerned only with getting the inflation rate at or below the target rate set by the Treasury. The inflation rate target is currently 2.0%, measured by the **Consumer Prices Index (CPI)**. Critics argued that the policy had a built-in deflationary bias. This is no longer the case, because the MPC is prepared to reduce interest rates to stimulate output and employment if it believes that on unchanged policies, an inflation rate below 2.0% will be accompanied by an undesirable fall in output and employment. In the words of the Labour government: 'The primary objective of monetary policy is price stability. But subject to that, the

Knowledge check 28

State one way in which monetary policy and fiscal policy differ.

Central bank The bank, usually owned by the state, which is in control of monetary policy.

Monetary Policy Committee (MPC) Committee set up in 1997, when the Bank of England was made operationally independent, whose main job is to set Bank Rate each month.

Bank Rate The Bank of England's official interest rate at which the central bank lends money to commercial banks such as Barclays.

Examiner tip

The Unit 2 specification does not require you to know about quantitative easing, but displaying some knowledge could add depth to an answer on UK monetary policy. Quantitative easing is an A2 topic rather than an AS topic.

Knowledge check 29

Name the main monetary policy objective and the main monetary policy instrument.

Bank of England must also support the government's economic policy objectives, including those for growth and employment.'

Using AD/AS diagrams to show how monetary policy affects the price level and real output

Before the short period from 2008 until 2010 when, in the fiscal stimulus, fiscal policy was used to stimulate spending in the economy, monetary policy rather than fiscal policy was used to manage the level of aggregate demand in the economy. To understand how monetary policy is used in this way, it is worth restating the aggregate demand equation:

$$AD = C + I + G + (X - M)$$

Whereas fiscal policy can affect aggregate demand by changing the level of government spending (G), monetary policy affects the other components of aggregate demand, C, I and $(X - M)$. An increase in interest rates causes the AD curve illustrated in Figure 14 to shift to the left from AD_1 to AD_2. (A cut in interest rates has the opposite effect.)

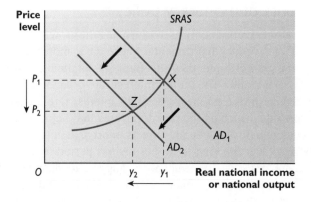

Figure 14 Raising interest rates decreases aggregate demand

When people are encouraged to save, they have less income available for consumption. Higher interest rates also cause businesses to postpone or cancel investment projects because they believe that higher borrowing costs make the purchase of capital goods unprofitable.

Linking monetary policy to the exchange rate and the balance of payments

The third way in which an increase in interest rates leads to a decrease in aggregate demand works through the effect of higher interest rates on net export demand $(X - M)$. A higher interest rate attracts capital flows into the UK. This causes the pound's exchange rate to rise, which makes UK exports less price competitive on world markets and imports more competitive in UK markets. The balance of payments on current account worsens, shifting the AD curve to the left. A cut in interest rates has the opposite effect.

Knowledge check 30

How might an increase in interest rates affect the consumption decisions of households with large mortgages?

Examiner tip

Practise explaining the various links in the chains of reasoning through which an initial change in the rate of interest affects C, I or $(X - M)$, and then the level of aggregate demand in the economy.

Knowledge check 31

How do lower interest rates affect the current account of the balance of payments?

AQA AS Economics

Examination skills

The skills most likely to be tested by objective-test and data-response questions on monetary policy are as follows:
- Defining monetary policy and distinguishing it from fiscal policy.
- Relating monetary policy to the objectives of macroeconomic policy, particularly the control of inflation.
- Explaining how monetary policy affects aggregate demand.
- Illustrating the effects of monetary policy with an *AD/AS* diagram.
- Explaining and evaluating recent and current UK monetary policy.

Examination questions

You should expect up to three objective-test questions on the terms and concepts listed in specification section 3.2.4 on this topic, although only one or two may focus exclusively on monetary policy. OTQ 8 in the Questions and Answers section of this Guide is a typical example. DRQ 3 tests knowledge and understanding of the nature of UK monetary policy.

Common examination errors

Commonly made mistakes on monetary policy include the following:
- Confusing monetary policy with both fiscal policy and supply-side policy.
- Treating monetarism and monetary policy as interchangeable terms.
- Confusing the instruments and objectives of monetary policy.
- Inability to use an *AD/AS* diagram to illustrate the impact of monetary policy on the national economy.
- Failure to understand how monetary policy affects the exchange rate, and how the exchange rate affects monetary policy.
- Failure to appreciate that the rate of interest is the key instrument in monetary policy.
- Confusing the roles of the government and the Bank of England respectively in setting the objectives and implementing monetary policy.

Summary

- Monetary policy is the part of a government's economic policy aimed at achieving the government's economic objectives through the use of the monetary instruments.

- In the UK, monetary policy is implemented by the country's central bank, the Bank of England, but aims to hit an inflation rate target set by the government.

- The Bank of England's interest rate, called Bank Rate, is the main monetary policy instrument in the UK. Bank Rate is set each month by the Monetary Policy Committee of the Bank of England.

- From 2009 until 2010, quantitative easing was used to supplement interest policy, but knowledge of QE is not required at AS level.

- Monetary policy is used to manage aggregate demand in a way consistent with achieving the monetary policy target set by the government.

- Raising or lowering interest rates affects C, I and $(X - M)$ and hence the position of the AD curve.

- From 2008 until at least 2011 monetary policy has been used to help the UK recover from recession, and during this period the inflation rate target was largely ignored.

Supply-side policies

These notes relate to AQA specification section 3.2.4 and prepare you to answer AQA examination questions on:

- the meaning of supply-side policies
- supply-side fiscal policy
- other main features of UK supply-side policy
- the impact of supply-side policy on the national economy
- the private sector's role in improving the supply side of the economy

Essential information

The meaning of supply-side policies

Before the 1980s, macroeconomic policy generally meant demand management. However, in the 1980s and 1990s, economic policy switched away from the demand side to the supply side of the economy. Economists now generally agree that, except in recessions, the major problems facing the UK economy are the supply-side problems of producing goods and services that are both quality competitive and price competitive in domestic and export markets.

Supply-side policies are a response to increasingly fierce international competition and they aim to change the underlying structure of the economy. Supply-side policies, such as tax changes designed to change personal incentives, may increase potential output and improve the underlying trend rate of economic growth. Supply-side policies also affect the level of unemployment, the inflation rate, and UK external performance as reflected in the balance of payments.

Supply-side policies are both microeconomic and macroeconomic

Many supply-side policies are microeconomic rather than macroeconomic, since they act on the motivation and efficiency of individual economic agents to improve economic performance. If successful, such policies also have a macroeconomic effect by shifting the economy's long-run aggregate supply curve to the right.

Supply-side fiscal policy

Before 2008, supply-side fiscal policy largely replaced demand-side fiscal policy. (Monetary policy rather than fiscal policy was used to manage aggregate demand.) Between 1979 and the early 2000s, successive UK governments cut income tax rates on a number of occasions. However, governments did this, not for Keynesian reasons to stimulate aggregate demand, but to create **supply-side incentives** in the economy. Supply-side economists believe that income tax cuts create incentives to work harder, to be entrepreneurial and to take financial risks, to save and to invest in new capital equipment.

Other parts of supply-side fiscal policy have been:

- **reducing state welfare benefits** to create an incentive to choose low-paid employment rather than unemployment

Knowledge check 32

What is the main difference between demand-side and supply-side economic policy?

Examiner tip

Always remember that fiscal policy can be used in a supply-side way as well as for managing the level of aggregate demand in the economy.

- **granting special tax privileges for savings**
- **reducing public spending, budget deficits and government borrowing** to free resources for private sector use. Supply-side economists believe that the public sector is too big and that it 'crowds out' the private sector. Cutting the size of the public sector and its need to borrow will 'crowd in' the private sector

Other main features of UK supply-side policy

Supply-side policies, other than supply-side fiscal policy, can be grouped into three main categories.

Industrial policy measures include:
- privatisation — the sale or transfer of assets such as nationalised industries from the public sector to the private sector
- marketisation — the shifting of economic activity from non-market provision financed by taxation to market provision
- deregulation — the removal of previously imposed regulations in order to promote competition by removing barriers to market entry and to get rid of unnecessary red tape and bureaucracy, which raise firms' costs

Labour market measures include:
- increasing labour market flexibility by reducing the powers of trade unions and replacing jobs for life with short-term labour contracts
- improving the training of labour

Financial market and capital market measures include:
- deregulating financial markets to create greater competition and lower borrowing costs (the financial crisis of 2007–8 may result in policy reversal here)
- encouraging saving by selling government-owned shares in privatised industries to encourage wider share ownership

Using AD/AS diagrams to analyse supply-side policies

To recap, supply-side policies aim to shift the economy's long-run aggregate supply curve (*LRAS*) curve to the right, thereby increasing the economy's potential level of output. The effect of successful supply-side fiscal policy on the *LRAS* curve is shown in Figure 15. (Note that an outward movement of the economy's production possibility frontier can also illustrate the intended effect of supply-side policies.)

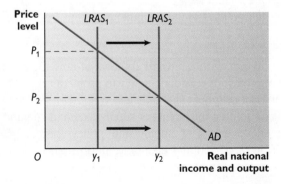

Figure 15 Supply-side policies shifting the *LRAS* curve to the right

Knowledge check 33

Why do supply-side economists support income tax cuts?

Industrial policy
Government policy which tries to make industries and markets perform more competitively and efficiently.

Knowledge check 34

Why is productivity important for supply-side economists?

Financial market
A market in financial assets or securities, e.g. the market in government bonds.

Capital market
A financial market in which businesses raise capital to finance their growth, e.g. the market in which companies issue and sell new shares.

Examiner tip
The mark schemes for
ECON 2 data-response
questions usually reward
relevant and accurate
explanation and evaluation
of supply-side policies.

Figure 15 illustrates another possible result of successful supply-side policy, namely a **'good deflation'**. Supply-side policies can lead to an outcome in which invention and innovation reduce business costs (and thence the price level) at the same time as promoting economic growth and higher levels of output and employment. In Figure 15, the increase in long-run aggregate supply causes real output to rise from y_1 to y_2, and the price level to fall from P_1 to P_2.

The impact of supply-side policy on the national economy

From 1992 until 2008, the UK economy benefited from continuous economic growth. Many economists argued that, by making markets more efficient and competitive, supply-side policies were vital in promoting and elongating the boom years. Such economists subscribed to the dictum 'first the pain and then the gain'. The pain was high unemployment and widening income inequalities, which were blamed on supply-side policies in their early years. The gain was the continuous economic growth that then kicked in, once the appropriate supply-side conditions were in place.

However, other conditions may also have improved national economic performance. These included the success of monetary policy in managing demand, and perhaps 'luck' in the form of benign conditions in an increasingly globalised world economy. Whichever view is correct, supply-side policies have widened income inequalities, although most of the growing inequality may result more from the adverse effects of **globalisation** than from supply-side policies *per se*.

The private sector's role in improving the supply side of the economy

Knowledge check 35
What is meant by the
supply-side 'crowding in'?

Supply-side policy is almost always pro-market and anti-interventionist. It attempts to change the function of government from provider to enabler. Supply-side policies aim to promote entrepreneurship and popular capitalism, replacing the **dependency culture** and statism which — for the supply-siders — are the legacy of previous demand-side economic policy. But supply-side policy cannot deliver unless the private sector does its job in improving labour productivity, innovation and investment.

Examination skills

The skills most likely to be tested by objective-test and data-response questions on supply-side policies are as follows:
- Defining supply-side policies and distinguishing them from other instruments of economic policy.
- Identifying a range of supply-side policies.
- Relating supply-side policy to free-market views of how the economy works and the appropriate approach of economic policy to problems posed by the economy.
- Illustrating the impact of supply-side policies on an *AD/AS* diagram.
- Comparing and contrasting the effects of supply-side and demand-side policies.
- Evaluating the effectiveness of supply-side policy, perhaps with the aid of appropriate indicators of national economic performance, such as productivity figures.

Examination questions

You should expect up to three objective-test questions on the terms and concepts listed in specification section 3.2.4 on this topic. OTQ 9 in the Questions and Answers section of this Guide is a typical example. Supply-side policies are relevant for discussion and evaluation of the issues posed in DRQs 2 and 5.

Common examination errors

Commonly made mistakes on supply-side policies include the following:
- Confusing supply-side and demand-side policies.
- Confusing supply-side policies with controlling the money supply (which is monetary policy).
- Failure to realise that some, but not all, fiscal policies are examples of supply-side policies.
- Inaccurate drawing of *AD/AS* diagrams to illustrate the impact of supply-side policies.
- Confusing interventionist supply-side policies such as nationalisation with anti-interventionist supply-side policies such as privatisation.
- Failure to analyse and evaluate properly the effects of supply-side policies.

Summary

- Supply-side policies are government economic policies which aim to improve the efficiency and competitiveness of the markets which make up the economy.
- Supply-side economists generally oppose Keynesian demand management policies.
- Supply-side economists are pro-free market and wish to reduce the size of the public sector.
- Supply-side policies can be both macroeconomic and microeconomic.

- Successful macroeconomic supply-side policies shift the *LRAS* curve to the right, and shift the economy's production possibility frontier outward.
- Supply-side fiscal policy is the most important part of supply-side macroeconomic policy.
- Privatisation and deregulation are examples of supply-side microeconomic policy.

Evaluating national economic performance

These notes relate in particular to AQA specification section 3.2.1 and more generally to the whole specification, and prepare you to answer AQA examination questions which require an understanding of:
- the meaning of national economic performance
- the role of performance indicators in the setting of macroeconomic policy
- the recent performance of the UK economy
- the future performance of the UK economy

Essential information

The meaning of national economic performance

If you refer back to pages 8, 9 and 26, you will see that economists have generally agreed that there are five, or possibly four, major objectives of macroeconomic policy, although there has been some dispute about the ranking. The five objectives are: full employment (or low unemployment), economic growth, a fair distribution of income and wealth, controlling inflation, and attaining a satisfactory balance of payments. The extent to which the macroeconomic policy objectives can be achieved provides a measure of **national economic performance**. Perhaps the most fruitful way of thinking about national economic performance is to judge the economy's past and current record on the macroeconomic policy objectives in terms of:

- reducing and then maintaining a low level of unemployment
- achieving and then sustaining a satisfactory rate of economic growth, uninterrupted by excessive upswings and downturns in the economic cycle
- avoiding excessive inequality in the distribution of income and wealth
- controlling inflation and avoiding destabilising swings in the inflation rate
- improving the competitiveness in international markets of the country's industries

The role of performance indicators in setting macroeconomic policy

An economic performance indicator, such as information about labour productivity and productivity gaps (the difference between labour productivity in this country and in competitor countries), can be used for comparing the performance of the UK economy with that of competitor countries. Performance indicators can be divided into lead and lag indicators.

Lead indicators

Lead indicators provide information about the likely future state of the economy. Surveys of business confidence and investment intentions indicate the existence of a feel-good or feel-bad factor and provide information about the likely state of aggregate demand a few months ahead. Statistics for house-building starts and holiday bookings also provide information about future spending, while data on commodity and input prices can signal future changes in consumer price inflation.

Lag indicators

By contrast, **lag indicators** provide information about the extent to which past economic performance has led to an outcome that meets or fails to meet the different criteria listed earlier for macroeconomic performance. Data on the level of GDP, and current and recent employment and unemployment are lag indicators that provide information about current and recent economic performance. The usefulness of a performance indicator depends, of course, on whether it provides accurate information about the state of the economy. Performance indicators are almost always presented in the form of statistical data: for example, unemployment and growth figures in the case of lagged indicators, and projections about the number of house-building starts in the case of lead indicators. The accuracy of the information provided by

Knowledge check 36

Is there a difference between national economic performance and macroeconomic performance?

Performance indicator
Provides information on past, current or likely future economic performance.

Knowledge check 37

Name one lead indicator and one lag indicator in addition to those stated here.

performance and **policy indicators** is thus highly dependent on the accuracy of the statistics available from the government and other sources.

Policy indicators These give policy-makers information on whether economic policy is on course to fulfil its objectives. Information about the money supply would be a policy indicator.

How far back must you go in your knowledge of UK economic performance?

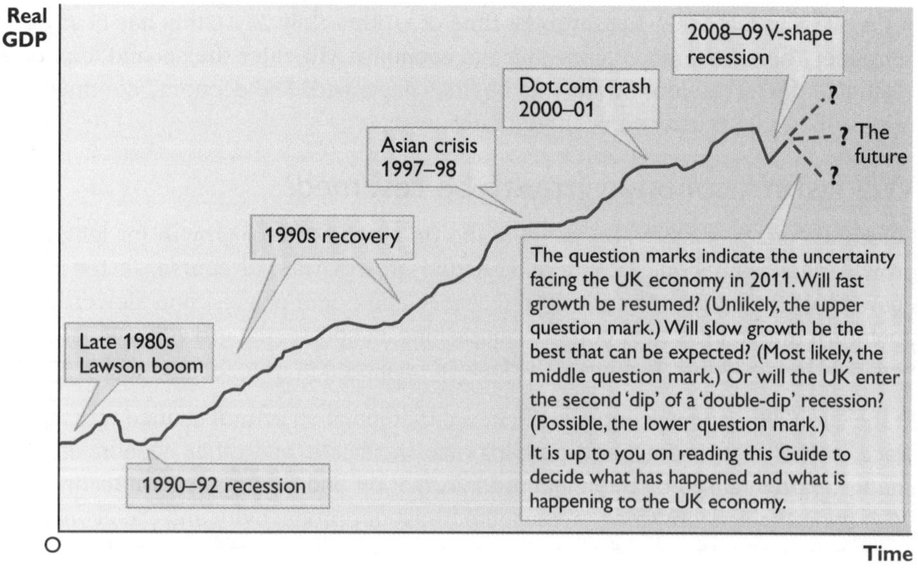
Real GDP
O
Time
Late 1980s Lawson boom
1990–92 recession
1990s recovery
Asian crisis 1997–98
Dot.com crash 2000–01
2008–09 V-shape recession
? The future
?
?
The question marks indicate the uncertainty facing the UK economy in 2011. Will fast growth be resumed? (Unlikely, the upper question mark.) Will slow growth be the best that can be expected? (Most likely, the middle question mark.) Or will the UK enter the second 'dip' of a 'double-dip' recession? (Possible, the lower question mark.)
It is up to you on reading this Guide to decide what has happened and what is happening to the UK economy.

Figure 16 The UK's economic performance, late 1980s to 2009

Although data-response questions in the ECON 2 examination on The National Economy are likely to reflect the state of the UK economy from about 18 months to 2 years before the date of the examination, the Unit 2 specification advises that information from earlier years may also be included. To answer questions well, you must possess knowledge of the performance of the UK economy over the 10 or so years before the examination and also possess some knowledge extending back further about the economic cycle. You must also be aware of the state of the economy at the time of the examination and the possible state of the economy up to 3 or 4 years ahead. Such knowledge is especially useful when the data in the question include a projection or forecast for future years, such as future levels of output and employment. The final part of an ECON 2 data-response question might ask for a discussion of the implications of the data for future economic policy or economic activity.

UK economic performance from the 1980s to the present day

Figure 16 shows how UK national output changed between the late 1980s and 2011. The graph illustrates several occurrences over this period:

- Boom conditions of the late 1980s came to an end in 1990. This period is often called the Lawson boom, after the then Chancellor of the Exchequer, Nigel Lawson, who, through expansionary policies, launched a period of fast economic growth.
- Severe **recession** from 1990 to 1992.
- Continued economic growth through the rest of the 1990s.
- Slowdown in 1997 and 1998, caused partly by crisis and recession in southeast Asia.

Recession Different economies define this differently. In the UK, the government's definition is falling real output (negative economic growth) for 6 months or more (two quarters or more).

- Renewed growth followed by a slowdown again in 2001, triggered by the dot.com crash.
- Recovery in the 2000s followed the dot.com crash and uncertainty due to the 9/11 terrorist crisis in 2001.
- Growth slowed in 2007, becoming negative in 2008 when the UK economy entered recession.
- Recovery in late 2009, but until the time of writing (July 2011), this has been very fragile. There have been fears that the economy will enter the second 'dip' of a 'double dip' recession. So far this has not happened. The economy continues to grow, but only at a very low annual rate.

Knowledge check 38

Name the different phases of the economic cycle or business cycle.

Will faster economic growth be resumed?

Before the onset of recession in 2008, the UK's trend rate of growth (or long-term growth rate) was about 2.2% a year. Actual growth was, of course, faster in the upswing of the economic cycle (the recovery and boom phases) and slower in the downturn that follows the boom. (In recessions, of course, the growth rate becomes negative, but as Figure 16 shows, the last UK recession prior to 2008 ended in 1992.)

In the late 1990s, some economists believed that major structural change was taking place in the US economy, and perhaps also in the UK and other economies. The change, partly caused by the impact of information and communication technology (ICT) upon the economy, had increased both labour productivity and the economy's trend rate of growth. The term 'new economy' was coined. Extreme optimists went further, arguing not only that future growth would be faster, but that the threat of a future recession had disappeared. However, the period of extreme optimism was short-lived. In the light of the deep recession that hit the UK economy in 2008 and the continuing world financial crisis, few if any economists now believe that, with recession apparently ended, fast growth will resume. At best, very slow growth is now expected. Emerging market countries, such as China and India, are of course growing fast.

What does the future hold for the UK economy?

As noted, after many years of continuous growth, the UK economy suffered a long and deep recession from the third quarter of 2008 until the fourth quarter of 2009. A weak recovery has since occurred, though the first figures released by the Office for National Statistics for the last quarter of 2010 showed the economy slipping back into negative economic growth, matched by slow growth in the first quarter of 2011.

The sovereign debt problem

Examiner tip

The terms 'sovereign debt' and the 'national debt' are not in the Unit 2 specification, but it is useful to be aware of them so you understand the problems facing the UK economy today.

One of the biggest issues hampering the UK's return to faster economic growth is the recently emerged problem of **sovereign debt**. This is a newly coined term for the **national debt** or government debt. Each year that the government runs a budget deficit, the *flow* of new government borrowing required to finance the deficit adds to the *stock* of national debt. Until recently, most economists did not think sovereign debt posed a problem. The debt was relatively small and could easily be financed. Historically, successive UK governments borrowed mainly from their own citizens (i.e. from the UK private sector) and overseas borrowing was comparatively small. However, two factors have now changed this, giving rise to the sovereign debt problem. First, the size of the budget deficit rose dramatically during the 2008 recession, as did the national debt. More borrowing is now needed to finance the deficit and to service the accumulated debt. Second, much of the extra borrowing is on international financial markets and these markets have become less willing to lend to the UK unless drastic deflationary action is taken to reduce the budget deficit.

Fiscal austerity

The Fiscal Policy section of this Guide describes how the brief **fiscal stimulus** launched by the Labour government in 2008 to promote economic recovery from recession was replaced in 2010 by tax rises and public spending cuts, i.e. by **fiscal austerity**. In part, this change in fiscal policy was a result of the new Coalition government's ideological dislike of 'big government' and its wish to reduce the size of the UK public sector. In part, the new policy was forced on the government by international credit rating agencies that threatened to downgrade Britain's AAA credit rating unless a fiercely deflationary fiscal policy was adopted. The government feared that downgrading the credit rating would result in international financial markets refusing to lend to the UK government – except at prohibitively high interest rates. (This is what happened to Greece, Ireland and then Portugal.)

If fiscal austerity continues, the UK is likely to experience, at best, very slow growth extending into the future – unless (as the Coalition government hopes) lower tax rates and the reduced size of the public sector free resources for an entrepreneurial private sector to use. (See the reference on page 47 to 'crowding in'.)

The Bank of England's possible failure in controlling inflation

Accelerating cost-push inflation caused by the rapid rise in prices of oil, commodities and food, and by a falling exchange rate, has damaged the credibility of monetary policy as a means of sustaining an acceptable rate of inflation. If people believe that the Bank of England has lost control of inflation, and that the CPI inflation target is meaningless, **expectations of higher rates of future inflation** may develop, which could become self-fulfilling. (If people expect inflation to increase, they begin to behave in a more inflationary way, and their changed behaviour delivers higher inflation.)

'De-coupling' the UK economy from America

The 2008 recession was 'imported' from America, where a financial crisis induced by the partial collapse of the US banking system led to massive falls in confidence and in aggregate demand. However, at the time of the recession, the growing importance of 'emerging market' economies, particularly the Chinese and Indian economies, meant that part of the world escaped recession. In future years, with Asian economies taking over as the main engines of global economic growth, the health of the Chinese and Indian economies may protect western countries from recession. The questions arise: has the UK economy become sufficiently 'de-coupled' from the US economy to benefit from 'emerging-market' growth, and if so, in future can the UK avoid 'importing' another recession from the USA, or indeed from eurozone countries?

Knowledge check 39

China and India are members of the BRIC group of countries. Why are BRIC countries so significant in the modern world economy?

Examination skills

The skills most likely to be tested by objective-test and data-response questions on national economic performance are as follows:

- Interpreting and analysing data covering a number of years to detect trends.
- Separating cyclical and sometimes seasonal variations from the underlying trend.
- Calculating percentage growth rates, inflation rates, rates of increase of wages, etc.
- Detecting correlations, which may sometimes be lagged, between variables such as employment and inflation.
- Appreciating the existence of leads and lags in economic data and whether a particular variable best indicates future or past economic performance.
- Understanding the contribution of a particular economic variable, such as productivity, to national economic performance.

Examination questions

Some objective-test questions may include statistics relating to the performance of the national economy in the 10 years before the examination. You should expect up to five OTQs based on real-world data. An example of a statistics-based OTQ is provided by OTQ 10 in the Questions and Answers section of this Guide. Virtually every data-response question will contain data on the recent performance of the UK economy. Likewise, the DRQs will ask you to describe, explain and evaluate aspects of national economic performance, and to assess the implications of the data for future economic performance. The six DRQs included in the next section of this Guide illustrate what to expect.

Common examination errors

Commonly made mistakes on national economic performance include the following:

- Lack of knowledge and understanding of the performance of the UK economy over the 10 years before the examination.
- An inability to compare and interpret data relating to the UK economy and similar economies.
- An inability to detect important features of data such as the economic cycle.
- Failure to apply general economic knowledge to help interpret data about national economic performance.
- A tendency to assume the future will always be a continuation of the present.
- The use of words such as 'vast' and 'massive' to describe quite small changes in national economic performance.
- Confusing data about national economic performance presented in index number form with percentage data.
- Failure to see the connections between different indicators of national economic performance.

Summary

- The concept of national economic performance can best be understood in the context of the five main objectives of macroeconomic policy.

- The term 'macroeconomic performance' figures in a large number of ECON 2 data-response questions.

- Lead and lag indicators can be used to reflect national economic performance.

- Since 1992, the UK's national economic performance has been characterised first by continuous growth until 2008, then by recession, and finally in 2011 by weak recovery from recession.

- The likely future economic performance of the UK economy will be constrained by the sovereign debt problem, fiscal austerity and the extent to which the UK benefits or suffers from the growing importance of 'emerging-market' economies in the global economy.

- Performance will also be affected by the performance of the US and eurozone economies, and the extent to which the UK is still 'coupled to' or has become 'de-coupled' from these important parts of the world economy.

Questions & Answers

The ECON 2 exam

The ECON 2 exam is 1 hour 15 minutes long and has a maximum mark of 75. The exam paper contains two sections, A and B, both of which must be answered. **Section A**, which accounts for 25 marks (approximately 33% of the total), comprises 25 compulsory objective-test questions or OTQs. One mark will be awarded for each OTQ answered correctly. **Section B** accounts for 50 marks (approximately 67% of the total) and comprises two data-response questions (DRQs), labelled **Context 1** and **Context 2**, of which you should answer one.

The exam's assessment objectives

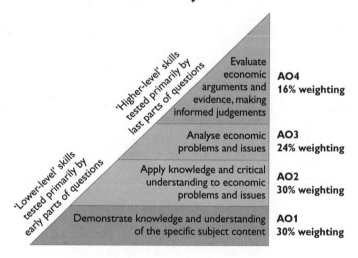

Figure 17 The examination's assessment objectives arranged along the incline of difficulty

The examination has four **assessment objectives (AOs)**, which are shown in Figure 17, together with their examination weightings, arranged in an incline of difficulty. 'Lower-level' skills of knowledge and factual recall are included in AO1 (at the bottom of the incline). Moving up the incline, increasingly 'higher-level' skills feature in the AOs: application of knowledge and critical understanding (AO2); analysis of problems (AO3); and evaluation of arguments and evidence (AO4). Overall, 60% of the examination questions are knowledge-based, testing the relatively 'lower-level' skills in AOs 1 and 2. The remaining 40% of examination questions meet AOs 3 and 4.

Answering objective-test questions

An objective-test question contains a 'stem' followed by four possible answers (A, B, C and D), only one of which is correct. Typically, OTQs are set to test students' ability to perform simple calculations and their knowledge of key definitions and concepts, especially on parts of the specification not covered by the data-response questions. OTQs primarily test the 'lower-level' skills related to knowledge and understanding in AOs 1 and 2. You should expect about ten of the 25 OTQs to test AO1, a further eight or nine to test AO2 and the remaining questions to test AO3, the analysis of economic problems and issues. AO4, focusing on the skill of **evaluation**, is not tested in the objective-test question section of the examination paper.

Answering data-response questions

Whereas the 25 OTQs in Section A of the examination paper are compulsory, Section B comprises two data-response questions of which you must answer one. As mentioned earlier, the DRQs are numbered as Context 1 and Context 2. Each Context question contains four sub-questions, listed as [01], [02], [03] and [04] for Context 1, and [05], [06], [07] and [08] for Context 2. The mark allocation for the four parts of each question is: [01] and [05] – 5 marks; [02] and [06] – 8 marks; [03] and [07] – 12 marks; and [04] and [08] – 25 marks. The total mark for each data-response question is 50.

The layout and structure of the questions will be similar to the six data-response questions that complete this Guide. Each question is likely to contain two or three sets of data. When, for example, three data sets are used in both questions, they will be labelled **Extract A**, **Extract B** and **Extract C** for Context 1, and **Extract D**, **Extract E** and **Extract F** for Context 2. In each question, one set of data is likely to be numerical, for example a line graph, a bar graph, a pie graph or a table. Text or passage data presented in AQA data-response questions generally resemble an extract taken from a newspaper article, for example an article in the *Financial Times*, the *Independent* or *The Economist*. Numerical data may be taken from a government source, which will be indicated below the graph or table used in the question. The Office for National Statistics (ONS) is a common source for numerical data used in an ECON 2 data-response question.

Both DRQs will be structured in exactly the same way and test the same assessment objectives. The questions are supposed to be equally difficult, but in practice almost every student finds one question more attractive than the other. Whichever question you initially favour, don't rush your choice of question. Careful thought and a sensible final decision are necessary if you are to do yourself full justice. You don't want to realise 10 minutes into your answer for Context 2 that you can't answer part [08] and that it is too late to switch to Context 1.

An 'incline of difficulty' will always be built into the DRQs, with the earlier parts of each question being the most straightforward. The first three parts of each DRQ will be marked using an **issue-based mark scheme** which lists the marks that can be awarded for the particular issues (and associated development) that might be included in the answer.

The last part of each DRQ differs from the earlier parts in three significant ways. First, and most obviously, parts [04] and [08] carry significantly more marks than the earlier parts of the questions — 50% of the total marks for the question and a third of the total marks for the whole paper. If you time the examination incorrectly and fail to develop your answer to part [04] or [08] beyond a cursory footnote, you will reduce considerably your chance of achieving a grade A. Second, whereas the earlier parts of the questions should be answered quite briefly, you are expected to write an extended answer of

several paragraphs for part [04] or [08]. You should think of this as a 'mini' essay. Third, 'higher-level' skills are expected. Because of this, a completely different type of mark scheme, known as a **levels of response** mark scheme, is used for the last part of each DRQ. It is vital to familiarise yourself with this mark scheme and to bear it in mind when you practise data-response questions.

The first two parts of each DRQ test primarily the 'lower-level' skills set in AOs 1 and 2. Parts [03] and [07] focus mainly on the 'higher-level' skill of analysis (AO 3). Finally, parts [04] and [08] test the evaluation skills embodied in AO4.

The four key skills

Knowledge and understanding

With respect to the two lower-order skills of knowledge and understanding, AQA requires you to show an awareness of economic terminology and theories relevant to the ECON 2 specification. You must also show awareness of real-world issues, especially those relevant to the UK. Your knowledge and understanding will be tested in the exam by most of the 25 objective-test questions in Section A of the paper. For Section B (the data-response questions) as well as for Section A, you are expected to understand macroeconomic theory, particularly the *AD/AS* macroeconomic model and related concepts such as circular flow. You must know about real-world performance of the UK economy, for example changes in UK growth, unemployment and inflation. Finally, you must understand how events in the global macroeconomy impact on the national economy in the UK, e.g. 'importing' recession from the USA in 2008.

Application

In Section B of the exam paper, the third part of each data-response question typically starts with the word: 'Explain'. Application requires the selection of an appropriate theory or set of theories from your intellectual toolkit to explain an issue or issues posed by the question. The issue may centre on the *causes* of an economic problem, or the *effects* of the problem. You are also required to apply your knowledge of current or recent events in the economy.

Analysis

Analysis requires selection of relevant information from the data source(s) and the use of this information, perhaps as evidence, in your answer. Information in the data is there to provide a *prompt* or *prompts* for the answer. You should indicate which bits of the data you are using, mentioning the Extract and the line numbers, but avoid just 'copying out' sentences or numbers from the data.

Evaluation

Evaluation is the higher-order skill which separates good answers that earn an A or B grade for the data-response question from those that at best reach grade C. Evaluation is also the skill which exam students find it most difficult to display.

To evaluate, you need to demonstrate a critical approach to economic models and methods of enquiry, for example the assumption that if markets are left alone without government intervention, free-market forces automatically produce economic growth and full employment. You should also demonstrate the ability to produce reasoned conclusions clearly and concisely and to assess the strengths and weaknesses of economic arguments and limitations of the data in the question.

Competing theories or explanations often lead into evaluation. Evaluation can require you to explain why, in your view, some arguments or lines of reasoning are more important than others. Where appropriate, alternative and competing theories and viewpoints must be weighed up. The assumptions you are making should be stated, considered and sometimes questioned.

The effects of different types of government intervention in the national economy must be judged, sometimes exploring the possible 'knock-on' and 'feedback' effects induced elsewhere in the economy. Very often, part (04) or (08) asks for consideration of the **advantages** and **disadvantages** of, or the **costs** and **benefits** of, or the **case for** versus the **case against** a course of action.

Good evaluation requires you to **prioritise** the evidence and arguments you introduce into your answer. One way to do this is to explain, when introducing each of the points or arguments you are making, whether in your view it is significant *always*, significant but *only under a particular set of assumptions*, or though relevant, rather trivial. When making such points, your answer must go beyond mere assertion, i.e. you must **justify** your arguments and use evidence.

Finally, there are two different ways of evaluating, but in my view the first way is better than the second. My preferred way of evaluating is to assess the strengths and weaknesses of each argument as you bring it into your answer. Is it relevant always, or only some of the time when particular assumptions hold? If you organise your answer in this way, make sure that every time you introduce a new argument you start a new paragraph. It is also a good idea to leave a vacant line between paragraphs so that the examiner's eye is drawn to the fact that a new argument is being presented.

The second way to evaluate is to leave it all to the final concluding paragraph. At its worst, so-called evaluation presented in the concluding paragraph can boil down merely to a statement such as, 'in my view, the case for is therefore stronger than the case against'. Unfortunately such a concluding statement is not evaluation, it is unjustified assertion. Good evaluation in a concluding paragraph must always refer back to arguments used earlier in the answer, making a clear final judgement as to which arguments, if any, are most important. Perhaps the best approach to organising your answer is to combine the two methods of evaluation, namely evaluate each point as you develop your answer before concluding with a winding up paragraph that presents an 'overview' or summary of the arguments you believe to be most important.

Finally, it is worth remembering that AQA draws students' attention to a significant distinction between **weak** and **strong** evaluation. Weak evaluation consists only of assertions unsupported either by evidence or by any accompanying analysis. By contrast, strong evaluation uses sound economic analysis to support the conclusions being drawn, plus evidence from the real world.

Evaluation and levels of skill mark schemes

According to AQA mark schemes, however good the analysis, an answer devoid of evaluation cannot climb above **Level 2** in the mark scheme (4 to 9 marks). Likewise an answer with some evaluation but no analytical use of economic theory is constrained to Level 2. (Such answers are sometimes called 'General Studies' answers.) A **Level 3** answer (10 to 16 marks out of the 25 available marks) must be a reasonable response, including some correct analysis but very limited or weak evaluation. A **Level 4** answer (17 to 21 marks) must include either some good and correct analysis but very limited evaluation, or reasonable analysis and reasonable evaluation. Finally, the highest level, **Level 5** (22 to 25 marks) requires both good analysis and good or strong evaluation, with final evaluation evident in a concluding paragraph

A strategy for tackling the examination

(1) On opening the examination booklet, turn immediately to the second section and spend up to 5 minutes reading *both* DRQs.

(2) Then go back to the first section and spend up to 20 minutes answering the 25 OTQs, completing your first run through the questions. While you are doing this, you will subconsciously be thinking about the DRQs.

(3) Read through both DRQs again, paying particular attention to whether you can write a good answer to parts [04] and [08] of each question, the parts that carry the most marks.

(4) After careful thought, make your final choice and spend about 50 minutes answering *all* the parts of the DRQ. Take account of the marks indicated in brackets for each sub-question when allocating the 50 minutes between each part of the question. Make sure you spend over half the time answering part [04] or [08].

(5) In the last 5 minutes of the examination, complete a second run through the OTQs and read through your written answers to check for and correct mistakes — including spelling and grammatical mistakes.

The exam questions in this Guide

The 16 examination-style questions that follow are designed to be a key learning, revision and exam preparation resource. There are ten **objective-test questions (OTQs)** and six **data-response questions (DRQs)**. Each of the ten OTQs is a typical question for one of the ten topics in the Content Guidance section of this Guide. Each of these questions is similar in layout, structure and style to an objective-test question in the ECON 2 examination paper. A commentary has been included after each question to explain the correct answer and any other important features of the question.

The ten objective-test questions are followed by six data-response questions. You can use the DRQs either as timed test questions in the lead-up to the examination or to reinforce your understanding of the specification subject matter, topic by topic, as you proceed through the Content Guidance. In this Guide, the data-response questions are numbered 1 to 6, but in the AQA exam you will eventually sit, the two questions will be numbered **Context 1** and **Context 2**.

This section covering the data-response questions also includes:

- A student's answer for each DRQ.
- Examiner's comments on each student's answer explaining, where relevant, how the answer could be improved. These comments are denoted by the icon ⓔ.

Understanding UMS marks

It is important to understand the difference between the two types of marks that the GCE examining boards award for students' work: **raw marks** and **uniform mark scale (UMS)** marks.

For the data-response questions, raw marks are the marks out of 50 awarded by the examiner who reads your script. These marks are added to the marks achieved for the 25 objective-test questions, to give an overall maximum total of 75 marks. After all the scripts have been marked, and basing their decisions only on raw marks, a grade-awarding panel decides where the grade boundaries should be set for each of the AS pass grades: A, B, C, D and E.

After all the grade boundaries have been set as raw marks, e.g. 55 out of 75 for a grade A, each student's raw mark for the ECON 2 paper is converted into a UMS mark. Uniform mark scale marks have the same grade boundaries — for all subjects and all unit exams. These are: **grade A: 80%; grade B: 70%; grade C: 60%; grade D: 50%; grade E: 40%.**

The marks awarded for students' answers for each of the DRQs in the following pages are raw marks and not UMS marks. It must be stressed that the actual raw mark at which a particular grade boundary is set varies from examination to examination, depending on a number of factors. The factors include: judgement as to whether the questions in the ECON 2 exam were relatively easy or difficult in comparison with the questions set in previous examinations; and the **statistically recommended mark** for a particular grade, which is determined by computer analysis of the marks earned at GCSE a year earlier by the cohort of students taking the ECON 2 exam.

Objective-test questions

Questions on **Topics 1 to 10**

ⓔ The ten objective-test questions that follow provide examples of questions typical of those set on each of the ten topics in the Contents Guidance section of this study Guide. Each OTQ is followed by a short commentary explaining the correct answer and any other matter relevant to avoiding choosing a wrong answer (known as a distracter).

Question 1: national income, economic growth and the economic cycle

Money national income for a country in 2012 is equal to:

A **the physical quantity of goods and services produced in the country in 2012**

B **real national income in 2012 adjusted for inflation**

C **the monetary value of the stock of capital and consumer goods in the country at the end of 2012**

D **real national income produced by the country's economy during 2012 valued at 2012's prices**

ⓔ Answer **A** provides a definition of real national income. However, the question asks for a definition of money national income. Money national income is real national income valued at current prices. Answer **B** is simply nonsense, while **C** invites you to confuse flows with stocks. **D** is the correct answer.

Question 2: aggregate demand and the circular flow of income

The diagram below shows the circular flow of income in an economy.

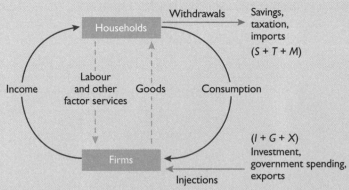

In the diagram, macroeconomic equilibrium occurs when:

A $S + T + M = I + G + X$

B **expenditure exceeds income and output**

C **all income is spent on consumption**

D **all goods are exchanged for money**

ⓔ Besides occurring at the level of real output at which $AD = AS$, macroeconomic equilibrium also occurs when leakages from the circular flow of income exactly equal injections into the flow. Statement **A** provides the latter definition and so is the correct answer. **B**, **C** and **D** do not define macroeconomic equilibrium.

Question 3: the aggregate demand and aggregate supply macroeconomic model

The diagram below shows a shift to the right of an economy's *AD* curve along its *LRAS* curve.

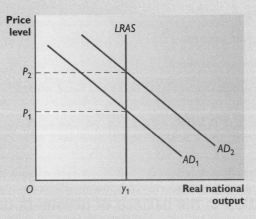

The diagram illustrates:

A cost-push inflation

B the movement to a new position of macroeconomic equilibrium

C the effect of successful supply-side policy

D the elimination of cyclical unemployment

ⓔ The correct answer is **B** as the economy moves to a new macroeconomic equilibrium at a higher price level, albeit at the same level of real national output. Cost-push inflation would be depicted by a leftward shift of the *SRAS* curve and a fall in real output. This is not shown on the diagram, so **B** is wrong. **C** and **D** are also wrong because successful supply-side policies would shift the *LRAS* curve to the right, while the elimination of cyclical unemployment would require the initial level of output to be below y_1.

Question 4: policy objectives and conflicts

Which of the following matched pairs of policy instruments and policy objectives makes most economic sense?

Policy instrument	Policy objective
A Income tax increase	Faster economic growth
B Increased government spending	Improved balance of payments
C Interest rate cut	More consumption and investment
D Interest rate increase	Lower exchange rate

ⓔ **C** is the correct answer: lower interest rates reduce the cost of borrowing and the incentive to save, thus stimulating consumption spending by households and investment spending on capital goods by firms. The other three policy changes would produce the opposite results to those stated in the three distractors.

Question 5: employment, unemployment, inflation and deflation

When the economy is in recession, which of the following is least likely to reduce unemployment?

A An expansionary monetary policy

B The Bank of England cutting interest rates

C Retraining schemes for redundant workers

D A new regulation extending employment rights for newly hired workers

ⓔ Statements **A** and **B** would reduce unemployment in a recession by expanding aggregate demand. Retraining schemes for redundant workers (statement **C**) might also be expected to reduce unemployment. This leaves **D** as the correct answer: an extension of employment rights would make it more costly and less attractive for employers to hire workers.

Question 6: the balance of payments on current account

Which of the following would be most likely to reduce a balance of payments deficit?

A Increased income tax and financial assistance for exporting industries

B A higher exchange rate and an expansionary fiscal policy

C An increase in the money supply and higher business taxation

D A boom in the domestic economy and a recession in export markets

ⓔ Increased income tax takes demand out of the economy, thereby reducing the demand for imports. Assistance for exporting industries obviously boosts exports. Statement **A** therefore provides the correct answer. All the events in the other statements would tend to increase a balance of payments deficit, with the possible exception of higher business taxation in statement **C**. Higher business taxation could go both ways. By taking demand out of the economy, higher business taxation could reduce a payments deficit. However, by reducing the international competitiveness of UK firms, it is perhaps more likely to increase a deficit.

Question 7: fiscal policy

Which of the following is an example of fiscal policy?

A **The Bank of England imposing controls on bank lending**

B **The removal of foreign exchange controls which restrict the transfer of currencies between countries**

C **The removal of regulations which restrict Sunday trading**

D **The creation of tax-exempt Individual Savings Accounts (ISAs)**

ⓔ **A** and **B** are examples of monetary policy rather than fiscal policy, while **C** provides an example of deregulation or the removal of direct controls on the economy. **D** is an example of fiscal policy and therefore is the answer. ISAs encourage households to save rather than spend on consumption because interest paid on the savings is tax exempt.

Question 8: monetary policy

Following an increase in the Bank of England's interest rate, the deficit on the current account of the balance of payments also increases. This is because the increase in the Bank's interest rate causes:

A **imports to fall**

B **the exchange rate to fall**

C **the exchange rate to rise**

D **exports to rise**

ⓔ An increase in the Bank of England's interest rate attracts capital flows into the pound, which increases the pound's exchange rate. This makes imports more attractive, but UK exports less attractive in overseas markets. As a result, **A** and **D** are wrong. **B** is also wrong, for the reason already given, which leaves **C** as the correct answer.

Question 9: supply-side policies

Which of the following statements about supply-side economics is correct?

A **Supply-side policies are used to improve the economy's efficiency and competitiveness**

B **Fiscal policy cannot be used as a part of supply-side policy**

C **Supply-side economists support the use of demand-management policies in all circumstances**

D **The main aim of supply-side policies is to increase aggregate demand**

ⓔ **A** is the correct answer, providing a neat statement of the purpose of supply-side policy. Supply-side economists generally oppose the use of Keynesian policy, so **C** is wrong. **B** is also wrong: supply-side policies do involve fiscal policy, although to create incentives rather than to manage demand. **D** is wrong because increasing aggregate demand is certainly not the direct aim of supply-side policy.

Question 10: evaluating national economic performance

The bar graph below shows annual percentage rates of change in real GDP (real growth rates) for the UK and other selected economies in 2004 and 2005.

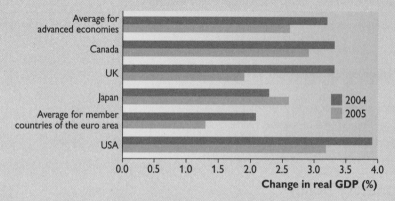

It can be inferred from the graph that:

A **UK macroeconomic performance was better than that of Japan in 2004 but not 2005**

B **in the UK, the annual rate of growth of money GDP was higher than the rate of growth of real GDP in both 2004 and 2005**

C **the UK benefited less from technical progress in 2004 and 2005 than the USA**

D **economic growth of the member countries of the euro area was, on average, lower than UK growth in both 2004 and 2005**

ⓔ The correct answer is **D** as the data show an annual growth rate in 2004 of approximately 3.4% in the UK compared to approximately 2.2% for the euro area average. In 2005, the UK growth rate was approximately 1.8% while the euro area average was around 1.25%. Economic growth is only one of the indicators of macroeconomic performance, so answer **A** cannot be inferred from the data. As long as the rate of inflation is positive, money national income grows at a faster rate than real national income, but as positive inflation cannot be inferred from the data, **B** is wrong. Technical progress is one of the causes of economic growth, but as it is not the only cause, statement **C** cannot be inferred from the data. Finally, as a general point, the growth rates shown in the data reflect the period several years before recession hit these countries. Real growth became negative in most, if not all these countries in 2008.

Data-response questions

Question 1 **Growth and recession**

Total for this question: 50 marks

Study Extracts A, B and C, and then answer all parts of the question that follows.

Extract A

Annual growth rate of UK real GDP and unemployment measured as a percentage of the labour force, 1990 to end of second quarter 2007

Extract B

Will the UK economy slip into recession?

In August 2008, analysts at the consultancy firm Capital Economics predicted that the UK economy would contract by around 0.25% in 2009. The forecast, which was the most pessimistic of any major City institution, sparked fears that the UK would suffer a recession similar in magnitude to that of the early 1990s.

Chief European economist Jonathan Loynes said he expected the economy to   5
contract for four successive quarters, starting with the current third quarter of 2008. 'We have long been more concerned than most other forecasters over the outlook for the UK economy. But three developments in particular have made us even more worried. First, the news on the domestic economy has been worse than we antici- pated. Second, the economy now looks set to receive less support from overseas   10
than we had hoped. Third, there is a growing danger that the downturn will be exacerbated by a contraction in bank lending to households and companies.'

The main driver of the UK slowdown will be a very sharp deceleration in consumer spending growth as households tighten their belts amid soaring bills and falling house prices. Another contributory factor will be much lower growth in UK investment spending thanks to rock-bottom business confidence and the effects of the credit crunch. Capital Economics said that it expected banks would continue to struggle to raise enough cash to restore their financial health in the wake of the credit crunch and housing slump, meaning they would continue to ration lending in the coming months.

15

20

Economists rarely forecast outright recession, partly because they are by nature cautious, and partly because such forecasts get disproportionate publicity, which influences consumer and business confidence adversely.

Adapted from news sources

Extract C

Is a recession necessarily bad?

Recessions have a number of bad effects, but some economists believe that in some ways recessions also do the economy good. By forcing inefficient and uncompetitive firms out of business, a recession may mean that, when growth resumes, the economy emerges 'leaner and fitter' and much more competitive. But many economists dispute this view, arguing that the costs of recession in terms of lost output and unnecessary human misery outweigh any alleged benefits.

Adapted from news sources

[01]   Define the term 'recession' (Extract B, line 4).   (5 marks)

ⓔ Part [01] or Part [05] of an ECON 2 DRQ always asks for a definition of a key economic term or concept. In every case, a short, sharp and accurate definition, often presented in a single sentence, is enough to earn full marks.

[02]   Using the information in Extract A, identify two significant points of comparison between the changes in the rate of economic growth and the changes in the rate of unemployment in the UK over the period shown.   (8 marks)

ⓔ The second part of a DRQ often asks the student to identify two significant points of comparison between the two variables shown in the data over the period shown. The data may be displayed in a graph or table. In this question the data are presented in two line graphs, one showing the percentage of the labour force unemployed and the second line showing the UK's percentage growth rate. When answering this type of question, it is important not to stray beyond the relatively simple task you are asked to do, namely to provide two points of comparison, supported by statistical evidence from the graph or table.

AQA AS Economics

[03]   **With the help of an appropriate diagram, explain two possible causes of recession in an economy.**

(12 marks)

ⓔ The third part of a DRQ on The National Economy sometimes asks a student to use an appropriate diagram to support the written explanation then provided. More often than not, the diagram should be an aggregate demand/aggregate supply (*AD/AS*) diagram, which is the key diagram you are expected to know.

[04]   **Do you agree that, despite its disadvantages, a recession is a necessary evil that an economy must learn to live with? Justify your answer.**

(25 marks)

ⓔ Sixteen percent of the total marks for the ECON 2 examination are given for the skill of **evaluation**, and almost all these marks are devoted to the final part of the chosen DRQ. The key instruction is likely to be 'evaluate', 'assess', or 'do you agree?' Evaluation is the skill that students find most difficult and which is generally necessary if a grade A is to be earned. In the AS examination, it is possible to achieve a grade A without displaying the skill of evaluation. However, to do this, you must perform very well in the objective-test part of the examination (which does not test evaluation) and in the first three parts of the DRQ. Generally, however, the students who can evaluate are the ones who gain the A grades.

Student answers

[01]   In the UK, the technical definition of a recession is negative economic growth (falling real output) for six months (two quarters) or more. **a**

ⓔ **5/5 marks awarded. a** This answer is precise and to the point and earns all 5 of the available marks. However, as the answer suggests, recessions can be defined in ways that differ from the technical definition laid down by the UK Treasury. So for this question, 2 marks could be earned for defining a recession in terms of an economic slowdown, or in terms of rising unemployment.

[02]   For the most part, the graph shows the percentage rate of unemployment growing when economic growth is also growing, and also falling when the growth rate later stabilises. Unemployment cannot of course be negative, but growth was negative in the recession at the beginning of the 1990s. There appears to be a slight lag in the data from 1990 to 1995, with the growth in unemployment preceding the increase in the growth rate. **a**

ⓔ **4/8 marks awarded. a** This answer contains three points of comparison, with the 'best two' being rewarded. Unfortunately there is no statistical backup for any of the comparisons, so only half the available marks have been awarded.

[03]   As already defined, a recession involves two quarters or more of negative economic growth. Most of the causes of recession lie on the demand side of the economy, which means that the causes of a recession are events that shift the economy's *AD* curve to the left. In my diagram below, **a** the *AD* curve slides along the *SRAS* curve from AD_1 to AD_2, with the end result that the position of macroeconomic equilibrium moves from full employment at *X*

(on the economy's *LRAS* curve) to Z, which is to the left of the *LRAS* curve. If the price level had remained at P_1, output would have fallen well below the full employment level of output (y_{FE}) to y_1. This would be the outcome if wages and prices are inflexible or sticky. However, if the price level falls to P_2 in response to the collapse in aggregate demand, output does not fall by as much, only to y_2. With this outcome the recession would be milder.

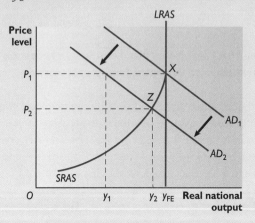

Two events that might cause the *AD* to shift to the left, thereby bringing about recession, are first, a collapse of consumer confidence, and second a fall in overseas demand for the country's exports. **b**

e **6/12 marks awarded.** The answer displays sound knowledge of recessions, but does not do enough to earn full marks. **a** Although the diagram is excellent, earning all 4 marks available for a diagram, **b** the written part of the answer mentions, but does not really explain, two causes of a recession. Only 1 mark is awarded for each cause mentioned.

[04] Recessions obviously affect an economy badly, and the deeper and longer the recession, the worse the effects. Since a recession results in an economy producing inside its production possibility frontier, potential output is lost and unemployed workers suffer from cyclical unemployment. It may be impossible to recoup lost output when the economy eventually recovers, and likewise workers, when they regain employment, may not be able to recover lost income and other factors such as lost pension contributions. Besides this, the unemployment caused by recession and the need to live off welfare benefits may destroy workers' self-esteem and lead to more crime, marital breakup and loss of social cohesion within the families of the unemployed. **a**

Another cost of recessions is known as hysteresis. **c** This is the name given to a cause of unemployment which emerged in the recessions of the early 1980s and 1990s. In earlier, milder post-1945 recessions, firms reacted to decreases in aggregate demand by laying off workers and by mothballing productive capacity. When the recession ended, firms quickly re-hired workers and brought idle capacity into production again. However, in the deeper and longer recessions at the beginning of the 1980s and 1990s, factories were often bulldozed and the firms that owned them completely disappeared. As a result, productive capacity declined, particularly in manufacturing and activities such as coal mining. When the economy recovered, demand had to be met by imports.

However, hysteresis brings me to a possible good effect of a recession, at least in the long run. Some economists believe that recessions are necessary as part of a restructuring process that, as Extract C implies, leads to the 'survival of the fittest'. Collapsing demand means that inefficient firms, and those that are slow to adapt to new conditions, such as Woolworths and MFI, go to the wall, while more efficient and flexible firms survive. And in a recession, conditions are created in which stronger firms either take over weaker competitors, or buy at rock bottom prices the assets of rivals that are forced out of business, e.g. the investment bank Lehman Brothers in September 2008. Viewed in this way, recessions are deemed necessary for the regeneration and survival of the economic system.

The latter argument is a bit like concluding that a plague is necessary to weed out the old and infirm in the population. While vulnerable people are likely to die, previously fit children and able-bodied workers will also meet their deaths. Likewise in a recession, many efficient and previously competitive firms are forced out of business, along with the less fit. A common cause of bankruptcy lies in the firm's customers failing to pay their bills, and in banks, who act as fair weather friends in a period of boom, refusing to extend loans as soon as their customers suffer a drop in sales. **b**

In conclusion, while I believe there is a little bit of truth in the justification I have outlined of recessions and economic downturn, I think that the disadvantages of recession are greater than the possible benefit. And the longer and deeper the recession, the greater the costs. Another factor to take into account is what is going on in the rest of the world. In the event of a global recession suffered by Asian countries such as China as well as by the UK, the eurozone and the USA, all would sink together. The effect would be devastating for all, but the UK might not lose competitiveness when compared to its rivals in world markets. However, if Britain alone enters deep recession (because of a problem that causes a decline in competitiveness that is unique to the UK), then when eventually growth is resumed, the economy will be even more uncompetitive because of lost investment and a possible decline in the quality of the UK's human capital. **a** In a deep recession, workers who lose their jobs may become less employable because their skills as well as their health decline. Recessions can trigger a vicious circle of decline in which firms lay off workers and cancel investment projects because there is no demand for their output, which at the next stage makes them even less competitive. **c**

🄔 **24/25 marks awarded.** This is an excellent answer that easily reaches the highest level in the mark scheme, Level 5 (22 to 25 marks). However, the answer does not quite merit full marks. **a** While the evaluation is good enough for full marks (being included as each argument is made as well as in the concluding paragraph), the answer is too thin on analysis. A relevant AD/AS diagram would have helped in this respect (or reference back to the earlier diagram included in the answer to part [03]): for example, to show how the destruction of productive capacity would shift the *LRAS* curve to the left. The student has obviously read beyond the demands of the AS specification, **b** which is shown, for example, by mentioning hysteresis — an A2 rather than an AS concept. Don't be put off by this; there is always a route to full marks in the mark scheme for students who make use solely of terms and concepts in the AS specification. **c** The concluding paragraph is good.

Scored 39/50 = grade A

Question 2 Investment, productivity and macroeconomic performance

Total for this question: 50 marks

Study Extracts A, B and C, and then answer all parts of the question that follows.

Extract A

Annual percentage change in output per worker, UK, USA and eurozone, 2000–2008

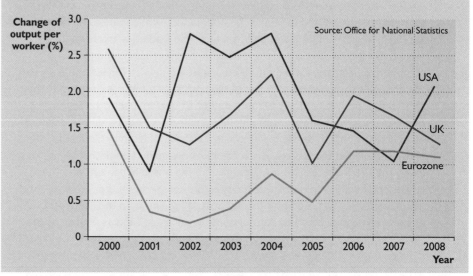

Extract B

A disappointing fall in UK productivity

The chancellor of the exchequer once said that productivity is the fundamental yardstick of macroeconomic performance. But a sharp fall in investment by UK firms and news that the UK's productivity is lagging still further behind its international rivals inflicted a double setback yesterday on the government's ambitions to boost performance.   5

Explanations of the UK's poor investment record include the heavy burden on companies of trying to eliminate pension deficits, worries over potential tax increases, and uncertainty over domestic and world economic prospects.

Economists believe that low corporate investment is a key factor in the UK's continued failure to raise its productivity performance. The latest international comparisons   10
from the Office for National Statistics yesterday showed that, measured by annual output per worker, UK productivity last year was 11% behind the average for other members of the Group of Seven leading economies, and 27% behind that in the USA. The productivity gap with the rest of the G7 was up from 10% in 2003, while the gap with the US widened from 24%. The gap with France narrowed a little, however.   15

John Philpott, chief economist at the Chartered Institute of Personnel and Development, believes that while about half of the UK's gap in productivity compared with the USA is because of low investment, the remainder is 'due in large part to inferior UK management practice, especially people management'.

Adapted from news sources, 2006

Extract C

The importance of information technology in raising productivity

It is now generally accepted that around 1995, after 20 sluggish years, American productivity growth began a remarkable surge. However, the advances in information technology (IT) and the dramatic cheapening of computing power that lay behind that surge have had much less effect on UK productivity.

The UK is not only worse than America at making IT hardware and software, it is 5 also much worse at using it. The Americans not only use much more IT per worker, but they also exploit it more effectively: even for a given amount of IT capital, their productivity is higher. That suggests British firms, at least, have not only fallen behind American practice, but also not even caught up with methods that Americans have imported to Britain. 10

Adapted from news sources, 2007

[01] **Define the term 'productivity gap' (Extract B, line 14).** (5 marks)

ⓔ The first part of each data-response question usually asks for a definition of a concept or term which is in the Unit specification. Occasionally, however, part [01] questions have asked for a definition of a term which is not explicitly stated in the specification. 'Productivity gap' is an example. Students often confuse a productivity gap with an output gap. Make sure you understand the difference between the two concepts.

[02] **Using the information in Extract A, identify two significant points of comparison between the annual changes in productivity per worker in the UK, the USA and the eurozone over the period shown.** (8 marks)

ⓔ The second part of a DRQ often asks for a comparison of two data series. Occasionally, as in this question, you are invited to compare changes that have taken place in three data series. Provided that the comparisons you make are significant and are supported by evidence from the data, a comparison of two of the data series will do, though compare all three if you wish to.

[03] **Explain two ways in which the UK's productivity gap could be closed.** (12 marks)

ⓔ Good answers to the third part of a DRQ often draw on 'prompts' provided in the Extracts. In this case, Extract B provides two prompts, namely the reference to low investment in the UK, and poor UK management practice, especially people management. It is of course possible to introduce explanation or analysis which is independent of any hints provided, but first it is a

good idea to look for any prompts, and then to develop the answer from these. The words 'data response' mean that you are expected to respond to the data!

[04] **Evaluate the view that investment in new capital goods is all that is required to raise productivity and improve the UK's macroeconomic performance.** (25 marks)

ⓔ Look out for 'weasel words' in the final part of a DRQ which ask you to evaluate. Such words are 'always', 'must', 'solely' and 'inevitably'. With this question, the 'weasel words' are 'all that is required'. If you agree or disagree 100% with the assertion in the question, you won't do very well. The skill is to adopt an 'it all depends' approach, in which agreement or disagreement depends on the assumptions you make when interpreting the question.

Student answers

[01] Productivity means output per worker, measured over a period of time, for example an hour, week, month or year. **a**

ⓔ **2/5 marks awarded.** Unfortunately the student has not answered the question. **a** The student has provided a good definition of productivity, for which the mark scheme allows 2 out of the available 5 marks, but has not defined a 'productivity gap'. A productivity gap is the difference between output per worker in two or more countries, each with a different average labour productivity. The most common mistake exam students make when writing about productivity is to confuse productivity with production.

[02] At the beginning of the period in mid-2000, output per worker was growing faster in the UK than in both the USA and the eurozone. It was growing by about 2.7% in the UK, but only by about 1.8% in the USA and 1.5% in the eurozone. **a** At the end of the period in mid-2008, the rate of growth of output per worker was higher in the UK than in the eurozone, but lower than in the USA. **b**

ⓔ **6/8 marks awarded.** It is worth stressing again that to earn all 8 marks for an answer to the second part of a DRQ, the student must make two valid and significant points of comparison, backed up in each case by statistical support. In this answer, the student makes two valid and significant comparisons (comparing data across the countries at **a** the beginning and **b** end of the data period), but only provides statistical backup for the first comparison. Hence 6 rather than 8 marks have been awarded.

[03] There are a number of ways in which the UK's productivity gap could be closed, but each is easier said than done. **a** An obvious method is to increase the rate of investment in new state-of-the-art capital equipment, so that each worker combines with more and better capital. **b** However, this will only close a productivity gap if sustained over a period of years and if the countries, currently with higher productivity, do not invest at the same rate. Closely related to this is a second way of closing the UK's productivity gap, by investing in and improving the quality of the UK's human capital. **b** This involves improving the quality of UK schools and universities and the motivation of both teachers and students. Again this is easier said than done.

ⓔ 12/12 marks awarded. This is an excellent answer which earns full marks. **a** Although the student failed to define a productivity gap in answer to part [01], this answer clearly shows that she understands the concept and does not confuse it with an output gap. An output gap measures the difference between the actual level of output in an economy (which reflects the current phase of the economic cycle) and the trend growth level of output. **b** The student provides two clear explanations of how a productivity gap might be closed.

[04] Investment in new capital goods is one of the factors that is required to raise productivity and improve the UK's macroeconomic performance, but it is not the only factor. But before I explain why, I shall first explain the meaning of macroeconomic performance. **a** Macroeconomic performance relates to how well the economy is doing at the macro level, in comparison to past performance or to the performance of competitor countries. For the UK, these are the USA, Japan and eurozone countries, though increasingly comparisons with 'emerging market' countries such as China are becoming equally relevant.

The UK's macroeconomic performance can be measured in terms of how well the economy is performing in relation to achieving the standard objectives of macroeconomic policy. How low is unemployment and is it unnecessarily high? Is the rate of economic growth acceptable and sustainable, and are the cyclical fluctuations sufficiently stable? Is inflation under control and the costs of inflation acceptable? How competitive are Britain's export industries and is this reflected in the state of the current account of the balance of payments?

Investment should be viewed as a necessary but insufficient condition for improving the UK's macroeconomic performance. Part of investment is neutral in this respect, namely the replacement investment that simply replaces worn-out capital goods. By contrast, the net investment that enlarges the national capital stock should improve macroeconomic performance. It should increase labour productivity and make the economy's industries more competitive in world markets. It should have the supply-side effect illustrated below of shifting the *LRAS* curve to the right and moving the economy's production possibility frontier outward. **b**

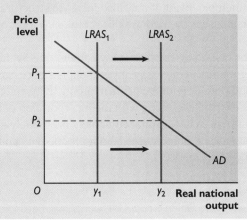

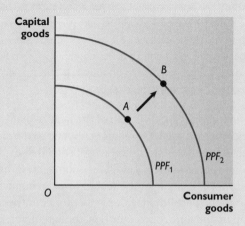

In my first diagram, the shift to the right of the *LRAS* curve, from $LRAS_1$ to $LRAS_2$, also brings about a fall in the price level (from P_1 to P_2). This so-called 'good deflation' could be another factor that improves macroeconomic performance. **b**

The extent to which this happens depends not only on the size of any new investment. It depends also on whether the investment involves more of the same, e.g. extra machines exactly the same as existing machines, or whether the new investment incorporates the latest technical progress and state-of-the-art technology. And there is also the possibility that new investment will be wasteful, e.g. investment in new machines or computers which businesses then don't use. This investment might reduce rather than increase labour productivity, if the new capital equipment gets in the way of workers doing their jobs properly. **b**

Successful investment in capital equipment that embodies the latest technology should lead to faster economic growth and also reduce wage-cost inflationary pressures. This should improve the economy's competitiveness. However, although investment more often than not creates new employment, it can have the opposite effect. It may lead to capital-intensive methods of production replacing labour-intensive production and the growth of technological unemployment. It may also increase structural unemployment if laid-off workers possess the wrong skills for the new jobs, or live in the wrong geographical locations. **b**

In conclusion, I shall re-emphasise my earlier point, which I have backed up with the arguments in my essay: investment is a necessary but an insufficient condition for improvements in productivity and macroeconomic performance. Nevertheless, along with the incorporation of technical progress, investment in new capital equipment is probably about the most important factor that increases labour productivity and enhances macroeconomic performance. **c**

ⓔ **25/25 marks awarded.** This is an excellent answer that does enough to earn full marks. **a** It is always a good idea when a question includes the words 'macroeconomic performance' to start the answer by explaining what this means. The student does this very well. **b** You should remember that the levels of response mark scheme for the final part of a DRQ does not require a student to meet every single one of the skills set out in the relevant section of the mark scheme.

The skills stated in the Level 5 mark scheme are:

Level 5 response	AO1: *Knowledge and understanding* of theories, concepts and terminology	AO2: *Application* of theories, concepts and terminology	AO3: *Analysis* of economic problems and issues	AO 4: *Evaluation* of economic arguments and evidence, making informed judgements
22–25 marks (mid-point 24) Good evaluation *and* good analysis	Good throughout the answer with few errors and weaknesses	Good application to issues Good use of data to support answer	Relevant and precise with a clear and logical chain of reasoning	Good with a clear final judgement

c However, it is important to note that to reach Level 5, it is generally necessary to finish the answer with a 'winding-up' conclusion. If the answer ends abruptly without a conclusion, it will usually be constrained to Level 4 (17 to 21 marks), however good the analysis and the evaluative points made.

Scored 45/50 = high grade A

Question 3 Monetary policy and inflation

Total for this question: 50 marks

Study Extracts A, B and C, and then answer all parts of the question that follows.

Extract A

The UK's annual inflation rate, measured by RPI, RPIX and the CPI, May 2007 to May 2008

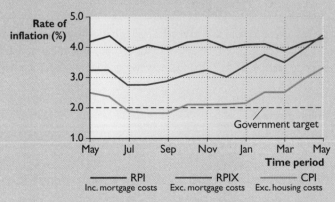

Source: Office for National Statistics

Extract B

Inflation once again rears its ugly head

In May 1997, the UK government gave operational independence to the Bank of England. For most of the next 10 years the Bank was remarkably successful in implementing monetary policy to keep the rate of inflation at or very close to the 2% target, measured by the consumer prices index (CPI), set by the government. Everybody agreed that monetary policy was extremely successful. 5

In 2007 and 2008, things began to change. The rate of inflation rose well above the target rate set by the government, growth slowed down and unemployment grew. People began to question whether the economic authorities, the Treasury and the Bank of England, were losing control over the UK economy.

Adapted from news sources, 2008

Extract C

There are hard times ahead

In a stark warning of hard times ahead, the Bank of England's Governor told MPs yesterday that there will be no growth in living standards for a year. Giving evidence to the House of Commons Treasury Select Committee, Mervyn King said there are going to be hard times ahead, and that living standards will not grow for at least a year. Families had to become accustomed to a 'one-year pause'. 5

AQA AS Economics

Household budgets will be squeezed by the rapid increase in the cost of fuel and food, while income growth will be constrained by the downturn in the economy. Borrowing will be made more difficult by the credit crunch, because banks are still reluctant to lend.

There is no 'magic shield' to protect the economy from the effects of a global rise 10 in commodity prices, and people must be persuaded that facing up to reality is preferable to trying to secure higher wage settlements in a vain attempt to protect their standards of living. The cost of winning higher pay awards will be a 'very prolonged and deep slowdown in activity'.

The Governor told MPs that inflation was 'likely to rise further this year', to beyond 15 4%, although the actual peak would depend on how much domestic gas and electricity tariffs increased. The relatively hawkish tone of his remarks helped to push the FTSE 100 share index down by more than 2%. Most analysts, however, took the view that an early rise in interest rates remains unlikely.

Mr King had earlier warned that the Bank's Monetary Policy Committee would 20 be willing to raise interest rates if that was necessary to dampen inflationary expectations, which have been rising, and to prevent an inflationary psychology taking hold in the labour market.

Adapted from news sources, 2008

[01] Define the term 'monetary policy' (Extract B, line 3).   (5 marks)

ℯ In recent ECON 2 (and ECON 1) exams, the term or concept you are required to define has usually involved at least two words – in this case 'monetary' and 'policy'. This may be the result of a deliberate attempt by the examiners to toughen or 'beef up' the question. To earn all 5 marks, you need to address both the words in the question.

[02] Using Extract A, identify two significant points of comparison between the rate of inflation measured by changes in the different measures of the price level over the period shown.   (8 marks)

ℯ Exam students often confuse the price *level*, with annual *changes* in the price level, i.e. in the rate of inflation. Always read the data (and the question) carefully to see if the question is about the price level or changes in the price level. Price indices such as the RPI and the CPI measure the price level, but changes in the index numbers over a 12-month period enable the rate of inflation to be calculated. The data in this question show annual percentage changes in RPI, RPIX and the CPI, i.e. the rate of inflation measured by annual changes in the index numbers for the three measures of the price level.

[03] With the help of an appropriate diagram, explain how a cut in the Bank of England's interest rate affects the rate of inflation.   (12 marks)

ℯ The '*logical chain of reasoning*' used in your answer could be: (i) explaining how a cut in Bank Rate (the Bank of England's interest rate) causes commercial banks such as Barclays to reduce

their interest rates; (ii) explaining how lower interest rates reduce saving but boost consumption; (iii) explaining how this shifts the *AD* curve to the right; and (iv) concluding that this increases the rate of inflation – though the extent to which this happens depends on the initial macroeconomic equilibrium and on the shape and slope of the *SRAS* curve.

[04] Evaluate the effectiveness of the monetary policy implemented by the Bank of England in recent years.

(25 marks)

ⓔ When a question asks about 'recent years', you should state how you are interpreting this term. Perhaps the best approach is to repeat the statement in the Unit 2 specification, namely that students should have a good knowledge of developments in the UK economy and government policies over the past 10 years but should be able to illustrate the economic cycle from the UK experience, taking as a starting point the boom of the late 1980s, followed by the recession of the early 1990s, and then the subsequent recovery (before the return to recession in 2008).

Student answers

[01]   Monetary policy involves the use of interest rates and controls over other monetary variables, such as the money supply, to achieve the objective of controlling inflation. **a** A central bank implements monetary policy — in the UK it is the Bank of England. Monetary policy can be used to achieve other objectives, for example preventing the economy falling into a recession.

ⓔ **5/5 marks awarded.** This answer is accurate and earns all 5 of the available marks. **a** The first sentence on its own would earn full marks.

[02]   Extract A measures the rate of UK inflation using three different price index numbers. Throughout the year, except in the very last part of the period, the rate of inflation measured by the general retail prices index (the RPI, which measures headline inflation) was higher than the inflation rate measured by the other two indices. (Right at the end of the period, RPIX, which measures underlying inflation, crept above the general RPI.) **a** Throughout the period, the rate of inflation measured by the consumer prices index (CPI) was lower than the rate of inflation measured by the other two indices. RPI inflation was just about 4.1% in May 2007, whereas CPI inflation was about 2.5%. A year later in May 2008, the RPI inflation rate was perhaps marginally higher than in the previous May at around 4.2%. **b** By May 2008, the CPI had risen dramatically to about 3.2%, which is outside the target range set by the government for the Bank of England to achieve.

ⓔ **8/8 marks awarded. a** With part [02] and [06] questions, it is always best to start the second point of comparison with a new paragraph, to make sure the examiner clearly sees that two separate points are being made. The student fails to do this with this question. **b** Examiners are given a certain amount of latitude when granting marks for statistical evidence. For example, the student would still have earned the available marks for stating that the CPI ranged from 2.3% to 3.5% over the period.

AQA AS Economics

[03]   A cut in the Bank of England's interest rate (Bank Rate) has the policy aim
of increasing aggregate demand in the economy, so as to increase the levels
of output and employment in the economy. The policy intention is not to
increase the rate of inflation, though this is a possible consequence if the
SRAS curve slopes upward to the right.

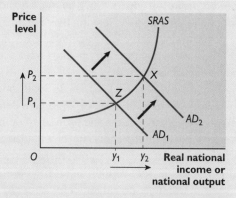

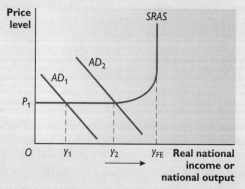

A cut in the Bank Rate reduces the interest rate commercial banks have
to pay when they borrow from the Bank of England. They in turn reduce
the interest rates they charge to households and firms that borrow from the
banks. The fall in interest rates leads to more consumption and less saving by
households and more spending on investment by firms. It is these factors that
shift the AD curve to the right from AD_1 to AD_2. As the top diagram shows,
increased aggregate demand causes real output to increase from y_1 to y_2,
though the extra demand also pulls up the price level from P_1 to P_2. However,
if the SRAS curve displays an 'inverted L-shape', as in the bottom panel of
the diagram, there would be little or no inflation and all or almost all of the
demand stimulus would end up in the reflation of real output. **b**

ⓔ **11/12 marks awarded. a** The diagram earns all the 4 marks available, though strictly the
time spent on the lower panel of the diagram and its explanation might have been better spent on
developing the answer to part [04]. This answer could well have earned full marks, but a mark has
been deducted for insufficient analysis of the process of demand-pull inflation caused by the cut in
Bank Rate. **b** A sentence or two on why consumption and investment increase, and more on why
the price level then rises is needed to gain the extra mark. Nevertheless, the student develops an
excellent logical chain of reasoning in the answer.

[04] As Extract B indicates, for most of the first 10 years of Bank of England independence, monetary policy was very effective in hitting the inflation rate target set by the government. The target was, and is, to keep the inflation rate (measured by the consumer prices index) within a band 1% above and 1% below a 2% inflation rate target.

During this period (from 1997 up to 2007), by raising and lowering its interest rate (Bank Rate), or indeed by leaving the rate unchanged, in virtually every month the government's target was achieved. The proof of the pudding appeared to be in the eating: the monetary policy target was hit, so monetary policy must have been successful!

In fact, during the successful period of the late 1990s and early to mid 2000s, monetary policy was used to manage aggregate demand. The policy was also pre-emptive. The Bank of England formed an opinion, based on evidence collected from data on the economy, of what the inflation rate would be about 18 months ahead if interest rates remained unchanged. If the data indicated that inflation would 'rear its ugly head', the Bank was quite prepared to raise interest rates at the time the judgement was made, to pre-empt or head off the expected rise in inflation. In my answer to part [03], I explained how cutting interest rates may create excess demand and lead to inflation. For this question, raising interest rates has the opposite effect.

One of the issues here relates to timing. If the Bank anticipated future events correctly, its policy would be likely to be successful. And the more successful that monetary policy was, the greater the benign effect on credibility. If people believe that the MPC is made up of wise men and women who always know what is happening in the economy, their behaviour is likely to be consistent with the Bank achieving its objectives.

However, even if this has happened in the past, monetary policy might only have been successful because other conditions were favourable in the economy. These included falling commodity prices in the early part of the period and the falling price of imported manufactured goods brought about by globalisation and the artificially low Chinese exchange rate. Arguably, supply-side policy was also a factor — first 'the pain' (of unemployment and labour market uncertainty) in the 1980s and early 1990s when supply-side policies were first implemented. 'And then the 'gain' in the late 1990s and early 2000s, when the UK economy was allegedly leaner and fitter with increased labour productivity and falling real wage costs.

My conclusion thus is that for the period of successful monetary policy, monetary policy was an important factor, but not the only factor, in controlling inflation. However, as Extract A indicates, in recent years, monetary policy has been much less successful. A main reason for this lies in the adverse 'supply-shock' which, in 2007 and early 2008, stemmed from the rising prices on world markets of commodities, food and oil. **a** These factors, over which neither the UK government nor the Bank of England has any control, triggered import cost-push inflation in the UK. Arguably, raising interest rates has little effect on cost-push inflation, though by creating unemployment it may weaken the power of trade unions to trigger wage-push inflation. It is also worth noting that if the general public see that monetary policy is ineffective in reducing cost-push inflation, the credibility of monetary policy may dissipate. Firms may then raise prices and unions (if they are able) may push for higher wage rates to try to prevent the erosion of profit margins and real wages that would otherwise occur. A wage–price spiral may be unleashed, which monetary policy on its own is ineffective to deal with. **b**

ⓔ **23/25 marks awarded.** This is an excellent answer, though perhaps it needs reinforcing with a bit more application of the standard *AD/AS* theory expected by examiners at AS. The student makes reference to the explanation in the earlier answer of how interest rates affect aggregate demand. **a** However, the answer would have benefited from explicit application of *AD/AS* analysis to the cost-push inflation and supply-side shock that are mentioned when explaining why monetary policy was less successful in 2007 and 2008. Knowledge, application, analysis and evaluation are strong enough, however, for the answer to reach Level 5. A little more precise use of theory would raise the mark to 25. One particularly good element is that the student evaluates each argument as it is introduced into the answer. The best answers always do this, rather than leaving evaluation to a concluding paragraph. **b** However, the answer ends with a strong conclusion, providing a further reason for placing the answer in Level 5. (Note: the question centres on inflation in the UK in 2008, when a commodity, food and energy price 'spike' triggered import cost-push inflation. A second and similar price 'spike' occurred in 2011, and may still be occurring when you read this Guide. The analysis and evaluation in this answer may also be appropriate for a question on more recent UK inflation.)

Scored 47/50 = high grade A

Question 4 **Wages and inflation**

Total for this question: 50 marks

Study Extracts A and B, and then answer all parts of the question that follows.

Extract A

Annual wage rate increases and inflation rates in the eurozone and the USA, 1996–2008

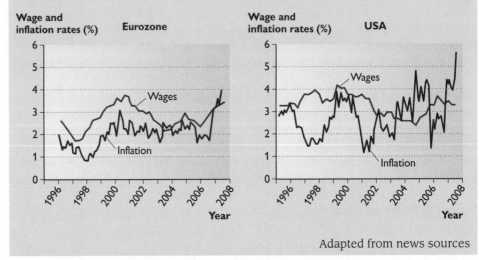

Adapted from news sources

Extract B

How European and American workers respond to inflation

In early 2008, consumer prices rose at their fastest pace in more than a decade in both the USA and the eurozone, fuelled mostly by cost-push inflationary pressures. Unlike in previous years, demand-pull inflation was much less significant.

The rise in the price level affected workers on the two sides of the Atlantic in different ways. Many European workers kept up with inflation better than their US   5
counterparts. Trade unions are more powerful in the eurozone countries than in the USA, and many laws and practices there are more worker-friendly. In Europe, generous worker protection often makes it more difficult to fire employees during a downturn, which tends to deter employers from hiring. As a result, unemployment rates have been markedly higher in the eurozone than in the USA.   10

In the USA, where trade unions are weaker and wages are generally not indexed to inflation, workers fell behind. Only 2% of US union wage contracts have clauses that tie wages to inflation.

What's good for Europe's workers could, however, prove costly to its economy. The eurozone currently faces a 'major risk' of a wage–price inflationary spiral. In 2008,   15
just 6% of polled economists believed that the USA faced such a risk.

But following the slowing down of Europe's rate of economic growth, workers in the eurozone may find it tougher in the future to keep pace with inflation. Rising labour costs can affect unemployment. The unemployment rate in the USA has been rising. However, in the eurozone, the rate is higher.   20

Central bankers in Europe and the USA are reacting to the wage situation differently. The European Central Bank (ECB) has kept interest rates high, while the US Federal Reserve policy-makers appear confident that a slowing economy will suppress wage growth. In mid-2008 they were expected to keep the Federal Bank's key short-term interest rate at the low rate of 2% to the end of 2008, in order to nurse the US economy 25 and financial system back to health.

Adapted from news sources, 2008 and 2009

[01]   Define the term 'demand-pull inflation' (Extract B, line 3).   (5 marks)

ⓔ A complete answer requires a definition of inflation, and the meaning of demand-pull. Although not required for this answer, you should understand that one version of demand-pull inflation centres on an excess rate of growth of the money supply creating excess demand, which pulls up the price level. This is the *monetarist* theory of inflation.

[02]   Using Extract A, identify two significant points of comparison between the changes in the rate of growth of wages in the eurozone and the USA over the period shown.   (8 marks)

ⓔ Exam candidates often confuse *levels* with *rates of change of levels*. If, for example, average wages rise during 2012 from £500 to £510 a week, £500 and £510 are the wage *levels* at the beginning and end of 2012, but the *rate of growth of wages* (i.e. the annual rate of wage inflation) is 2%.

[03]   With the use of at least one appropriate diagram, explain the difference between cost-push and demand-pull inflation.   (12 marks)

ⓔ The appropriate diagrams to use are both *AD/AS* diagrams. Cost-push inflation is illustrated by the effect of a leftward shift of the *SRAS* curve. By contrast, shifting the *AD* curve to the right illustrates demand-pull inflation.

[04]   Evaluate the economic policies that a government might use to reduce cost-push inflationary pressures.   (25 marks)

ⓔ Exam candidates often misread questions such as this one. In the first place, they wrongly interpret the questions as referring solely to a UK government, or indeed only the current UK government. In the second place, they ignore the word 'might', which is a key word in the question. The word 'might' allows you to discuss policies which have never been used in the UK, at least in recent times, e.g. making it illegal for wages or prices to rise. Note also that 'policies' is plural, so you must evaluate at least two policies, and preferably three or four. But don't write a 'shopping list' covering a large number of policies. The 'shopping list' approach leads to a superficial answer devoid of the analysis and evaluation in depth required to earn a high mark.

Student answers

[01] Inflation is a continuing and persistent increase in the average price level. Demand-pull inflation is the name given to a continuously rising price level **a** caused by excess aggregate demand in the economy. **b**

ⓔ **5/5 marks awarded.** This answer is precise and to the point and earns all 5 of the available marks. Both **a** inflation and **b** demand-pull have been defined.

[02] In the first half of the data period (from 1996 to about 2001), the annual rate of growth of wages was higher in the USA than in eurozone countries. For example, in 1996 wage rates were growing by about 3.2% a year in the USA, but only by about 2.7% in the eurozone. (However, the data series appear to start at slightly different dates.)

In the second half of the data series, the position was reversed. For example, eurozone wage rates were rising by about 3.6%, whereas the US rise was lower at about 3.2%.

Thirdly, at the end of all four data series, the rate of inflation rose above the rate of increase of wages. **a**

ⓔ **8/8 marks awarded.** Although students are required to identify two points of comparison, more than two comparative points can often be identified. **a** However, you should never waste time by comparing more than two of these. Only the 'best two' earn marks, in this case the first two comparisons. Although the student includes a third point of comparison, he does not lose marks. For all questions, positive rather than negative marking is used.

[03] Cost-push inflation, which is illustrated in the left-hand panel of the diagram below, occurs when the costs of production of businesses rise, for example because of increased wages, raw material or energy costs. The former could be caused by increased trade union militancy or by an adverse 'supply shock' hitting the economy, e.g. rising oil costs because of the effects of a Caribbean hurricane on US oil production. Monopoly power can also lead to firms passing these costs on to consumers in the form of higher prices, in order to maintain profit margins that would otherwise be squeezed. Whatever the underlying cause, the *SRAS* curve shifts to the left from $SRAS_1$ to $SRAS_2$. **a**

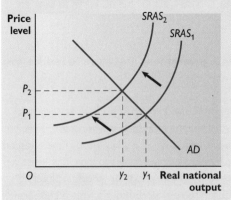
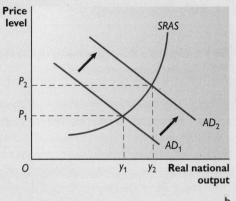

b

The right-hand panel of the diagram illustrates demand-pull inflation. An increase in consumption spending, caused perhaps by an interest rate cut (monetary policy), or a tax cut (fiscal policy), or perhaps by just a general increase in consumer confidence, shifts the AD curve to the right from AD_1 to AD_2. Firms are only prepared to produce the extra output to meet the increase of demand if the price level rises. In this way, the increase in aggregate demand pulls up the price level. **a**

ⓔ **12/12 marks awarded.** The answer is based on **a** an explanation of sufficient depth for each cause of inflation together with **b** two good AD/AS diagrams. The answer includes two logical chains of reasoning, going beyond merely stating that with cost-push inflation, the $SRAS$ curve shifts to the left, and that with demand-pull inflation, the AD curve shifts to the right. Note that the student has drawn two AD/AS diagrams. It is possible to earn full marks with both events on a single diagram. However, two are better for this question, as each one is clearer and easier to link to the written explanation. (Note: to invite two diagrams, the question states 'with the use of at least one appropriate diagram, explain…'.)

[04]   As I have already stated in my answer to part [03] **a**, cost-push inflationary pressure may emanate either from forces within the domestic economy, or from events in other countries and/or the global economy, or from a combination of both.

Over 40 years ago in the early 1970s, Britain suffered from both types of cost-push inflation. The internal or domestic cause resulted from the power of trade unions to force employers to increase the money wages union members were paid so as to maintain their real wages (the purchasing power of their money wages) at a time when rising oil costs etc. were forcing the general price level up.

Policies appropriate to reduce wage cost-push inflation include imposing a wage freeze, reducing the power of trade unions and deflating aggregate demand so as to reduce the ability of workers, and their trade unions, to force employers to grant wage rises higher than the rate at which labour productivity is increasing. Imposing a wage freeze and reducing the power of trade unions might require the introduction of tough anti-labour laws. This might cause strikes and a breakdown in social order.

Such policies, which were used in the past, may indeed have been successful because there is little evidence of wage cost-push inflation at the present day. The policies may also have been successful because workers' expectations of future inflation were reduced. This was achieved by establishing the credibility of the government's anti-inflation policies. If people expect inflation to be low, they will behave in a less-inflationary way, and inflation will end up being low!

However, to return to my earlier point, cost-push inflationary pressure may be caused by events in other countries, sometimes in the form of 'supply-side shocks' such as war in the middle east leading to a large rise in the price of oil. Import cost-push inflation results. Until recently the prices of most imported manufactured goods were falling. When this was the case, an effective government policy to prevent cost-push inflation was to encourage

such imports. Trade unions and their employers in the domestic economy are less likely to behave in a way that causes cost-push inflation if they have to compete with imported manufactured goods from China. However, this approach is most effective when the prices of imported goods are falling. In 2011 the prices of imported manufactured goods, as well as imported raw material and energy prices, were rising. In this situation, relying on the benign effects of globalisation to reduce domestic cost-push inflation may not work

Unfortunately, there is very little that a domestic government can do to reduce import prices, though it may use some of the policies I have just described to try to prevent imported inflation triggering a second round of domestically caused cost-push inflation. **b**

ⓔ **21/25 marks awarded.** This answer reaches the upper end of Level 4. The answer makes a neat distinction between wage cost-push and import cost-push inflation, considering a number of relevant policies, each of which is evaluated. To reach Level 5, the answer needs **a** more explicit analysis, using an *AD/AS* diagram, of cost-push inflation. Doubtless, the student thought he had done this when referring back to his answer to part [03]. However, from 2012 onwards, it is likely that the examiner marking part [04] will mark only this part and will not see earlier parts of your answer. It is therefore best to include all the analysis relevant to part [04] in the part [04] answer, even if this repeats what you say in part [03]. **b** To reach Level 5, the answer also needs a 'winding-up' conclusion.

Scored 46/50 = high grade A

Question 5 Fiscal policy and supply-side economics

Total for this question: 50 marks

Study Extracts A and B, and then answer all parts of the question that follows.

Extract A

UK taxes and public spending (% of GDP)

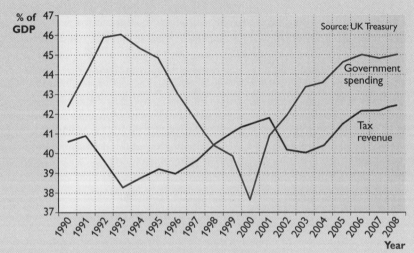

Extract B

Supply-side fiscal policy

When the Republican politician Ronald Reagan campaigned for the US presidency in 1980, he promised to cut taxes in what seemed, at the time, a magical way. Tax revenue would go up, not down, he said, as the economy boomed in response to lower tax rates. Far from getting larger, the government's budget deficit would fall in size.   5

Since then, supply-side economics has become a central tenet of pro-free market political and economic thinking. That's despite the fact that the big supply-side tax cuts of the 1980s and the 2000s did not work out as advertised, as even most supporters acknowledge.

But advocates see broader economic benefits from lowering tax rates, which is one   10
of the reasons that supply-side fiscal policy reappeared as a point of contention in the 2008 US election campaign.

'What really happens is that the economy grows more vigorously when you lower tax rates,' said Kevin Hassett, an adviser to the Republican nominee, John McCain, and the director for economic policy studies at the conservative American Enterprise   15
Institute. 'It is beyond the reach of economic science to explain precisely why that happens, but it does.'

Even with a growing economy, however, the promised boon in tax revenue may never materialise. 'If you are cutting taxes without offsetting the cuts through reductions in spending, then all you are doing is increasing the debt and postponing the taxes,' said Jason Furman, director of the Hamilton Project at the Brookings Institution, and also a policy adviser to Barack Obama, the 2008 Democratic presidential candidate.

20

Also, a main result of the tax cuts introduced by American administrations was that much more of national income flowed to rich households. The supply-side economists now argue that because the wealthiest Americans have so many ways to shelter their money from taxes, the incentive to declare more taxable income is much greater when tax rates are lowered. 'The supply-side argument these days really applies to upper-income people,' said Robert M. Solow, a Nobel laureate in economics who served in the Kennedy administration in the 1960s. 'They are portrayed as the golden geese, and you don't want to discourage them from laying their eggs.'

25

30

Gene Sperling, an economic adviser to President Bill Clinton in the 1990s, says that the supply-side economists vastly exaggerate the incentive effect of relatively small changes in tax rates while ignoring the benefits of bringing government revenue more closely in line with spending. 'The supply-side economists predicted in the 1990s that raising tax rates, even for deficit reduction, would lead us to recession,' Mr Sperling said. 'What followed instead was the longest recovery in history, and the people whose tax rates went up had exceptional income gains.'

35

Adapted from news sources, 2008

[01]   Define the term 'budget deficit' (Extract B, line 4).   (5 marks)

> ⓔ A significant minority of exam students confuse a budget deficit ($G > T$) with a balance of payments deficit on current account ($X < M$). Make sure you don't make this mistake, particularly in an answer to a longer part of a question. With a part [01] question you would miss the opportunity to gain 5 marks; with a part [04] question it would be 25 marks!

[02]   Using Extract A, identify two points of comparison between the changes in tax and government spending levels, as percentages of GDP, over the period shown.   (8 marks)

> ⓔ When you first look at a graph such as the one in Extract A, check whether the data are presented in billions of pounds or as percentages of GDP. Having checked how the data are presented, make sure you quote the units of measurement in your comparison.

[03]   Using at least one appropriate diagram, explain how tax cuts might affect macroeconomic equilibrium in an economy.   (12 marks)

> ⓔ As is the case in parts [03] of DRQs 1 and 3, the most appropriate diagram to draw is probably an AD/AS diagram. Macroeconomic equilibrium is shown on this diagram where $AD = AS$. With this question, however, a circular flow diagram would also be appropriate, with macroeconomic equilibrium indicated where leakages of demand out of the circular flow of income equal injections of spending into the circular flow, i.e. where $S + T + M = I + G + X$.

[04]   **Evaluate the argument that income tax cuts must be granted to high-paid workers if the rate of economic growth is to be increased.**   (25 marks)

ⓔ The 'weasel word' in this question is 'must'. With this type of question, always remember to question the word 'must' and to adopt an 'it all depends' approach to the question. Argue that, under different sets of assumptions, the answer may be different.

Student answers

[01]   A budget deficit is the difference between revenue coming in and expenditure flowing out. **a** For a government, its budget deficit, which is a flow, is the difference between the flow of public spending on items such as schools, hospitals and the wages of those employed in the public sector, and government revenue (which is mostly tax revenue). In the case of a deficit, as distinct from a surplus, expenditure exceeds revenue. A government's budget deficit is financed by government borrowing. **b**

ⓔ **5/5 marks awarded.** This is an accurate developed answer that earns all 5 marks, **a** although only the first sentence is needed to do so. When answering a question on a budget deficit, it is useful to understand that government spending, tax revenue and the budget deficit, which is the residual between the two, are economic flows, **b** as is the flow of borrowing with which the government finances its deficit. The stock concept that relates to the budget deficit is the national debt. This is the historically accumulated stock of borrowing which the government has not paid back. Each year, when there is a budget deficit, the government has to take out extra borrowing. Conversely, in the event of a budget surplus, the government uses its surplus tax revenue to pay off part of the national debt. However for a part [01] question, you shouldn't include all this information in your answer – you would be drifting into irrelevance.

[02]   For most of the years in the 18 or so year data period shown in Extract A, the government's finances were in deficit, with government spending growing to be higher than tax revenue.
     However, between mid-1998 and the end of 2002, there was a budget surplus, with tax revenue exceeding government spending. **a**
     The budget deficit was biggest in mid 1993, when government spending stood at about 46% of GDP, while tax revenues were 38.4% of GDP. The deficit thus equalled 7.6% of GDP. By contrast, the budget surplus was largest in mid-2000, when tax revenue at 42.5% of GDP was higher than spending (at 37.6%) by 4.9%.**b**

ⓔ **6/8 marks awarded. a** The first two sentences in the answer make a point of comparison, but the comparison is not properly supported by evidence. Two marks, but no more, could be awarded for the point of comparison. **b** The third paragraph compares the peaks of taxation and government spending and quotes supporting statistics, thereby earning 4 marks.

[03] Tax cuts can affect macroeconomic equilibrium (the level of output at which $AD = AS$) in two different ways, which are both shown **a** in my diagram below. The left-hand panel of the diagram shows tax cuts used as a *demand-side* economic policy instrument. By contrast, the right-hand panel shows tax cuts used in a *supply-side* way.

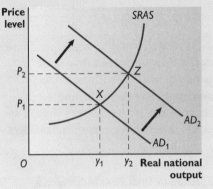

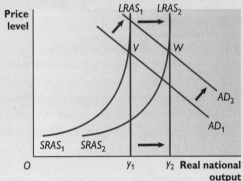

In the left-hand panel of my diagram, macroeconomic equilibrium is initially at point X, at the intersection of the $SRAS$ curve and the curve labelled AD_1. Real output is y_1 and the price level is P_1. Income tax cuts increase consumption, thereby shifting the AD curve to the right to AD_2. The new macroeconomic equilibrium is at point Z, with real output having risen to y_2 and the price level to P_2.

By contrast, the right-hand panel illustrates the supply-side argument that, through creating incentives to invest, save, work hard and be entrepreneurial, income tax cuts shift the long-run aggregate supply curve to the right (from $LRAS_1$ to $LRAS_2$). When drawing my diagram, I have assumed that the tax cuts also have a demand-side effect (intended or otherwise), illustrated by the AD curve also shifting to the right (from AD_1 to AD_2). The old macroeconomic equilibrium prior to the tax cut was at point V, whereas the new macroeconomic equilibrium is at point W. I have assumed that the increase in aggregate demand is just sufficient to absorb the increase in supply brought about through the supply-side incentive effect. Given this assumption, the price level has hardly changed (though I haven't included the actual price level in the right-hand diagram). Real output, however, has increased from y_1 to y_2.**b**

ⓔ **12/12 marks awarded.** This is a very good answer that earns full marks, but the answer is really too long. Much of the answer would be more appropriate for a part [04] answer testing the skill of evaluation, rather than for a part [03] answer testing explanation and analysis. **a** Full marks could be earned by drawing just one of the panels of the diagram, and then by providing a full explanation of the effect of the tax cut in the context of the chosen diagram. **b** The danger with this extended answer is that that the student then runs out of time when answering part [04], which carries 25 marks as against 12 marks for part [03].

[04] I shall start my answer to this question by expanding on the latter part of my answer to part [03]. The view or sentiment expressed in the question **a** is very much a supply-side view favoured by pro-free market economists, especially in the USA – though the UK chancellor of the exchequer, George Osborne, shares this view. Supply-side economists believe that high tax rates create disincentives, particularly in labour markets, and also for budding entrepreneurs. For ordinary employees, high income tax rates lead to a reduction in motivation and a refusal to work overtime. In extreme cases, high tax rates exacerbate a problem known as the unemployment trap. Workers end up trapped in unemployment, preferring to live off state welfare benefits rather than to supply labour in low-paid jobs subject to income tax and National Insurance contributions. At the upper end of the pay scale, workers are often internationally mobile. Arguably, high tax rates contribute to a brain drain through which investment bankers, doctors and the like move overseas to more friendly tax regimes. **b**

The question also implies that only high-paid workers should be given tax cuts. **a** In the interest of social fairness, if taxes are cut, then surely they should be extended to all workers. But as I have said, the tax cuts made in the USA over 20 years ago did not, as their conservative supporters had predicted, generate higher total tax revenues.

Supply-side economists believed that income tax cuts would boost economic growth, with the result that despite lower tax rates, the US government would end up collecting more tax revenue. They also believed that the rich people benefiting from tax cuts would do the decent thing and declare their income and refrain from indulging in tax avoidance schemes. However, total tax revenues fell rather than increased, and as a result the quality of public services available to the poor, such as Medicare, deteriorated. The poor became worse off in two senses: first, the rich rather than the poor benefited most from the tax cuts, and second, the quality of public services consumed mostly by the poor was much reduced.

Some people, myself included, cynically believe that the supply-side tax cuts that were skewed to benefiting the rich, were simply the reward offered by Republican administrations to the rich, who gave the Republicans campaign money and voted them into power. **c** As a Labour MP once said: 'supply-side economics is based on wealth incentives for the already wealthy and poverty incentives for the already poor. To incentivise the already rich, you must offer them more money, while to incentivise the poor you must threaten them with greater poverty if they refuse to work'. I agree with this view and reject the supply-siders' 'trickle down' argument that the poor benefit from the rich getting even richer because the rich can now afford to employ them as servants and gardeners.

@ **13/25 marks awarded.** After the quality of the answers to the earlier parts of the question, this answer is a disappointment. Though interesting to read, the answer only just reaches Level 3 (12 to 16 marks), which requires a 'reasonable answer, including some correct analysis but very limited evaluation'. **c** The answer is also too polemical (adopting a one-sided political stance), but more importantly, **b** it does not provide any real analysis of the key issue in the question, namely

the causes of economic growth and the role, if any, of tax cuts in promoting economic growth. Without proper analysis, evaluation tends to be weak, though **a** the answer does display the skill of application, i.e. making use of the data in the Extracts. The key word 'must' in the question is ignored in the discussion. Hence the answer only meets the Level 3 criteria, but no higher. On its own, this answer would not reach a grade A, but there is sufficient quality in the answers to the earlier parts of the question to merit a grade A overall.

Scored 36/50 = borderline grade A

Question 6 The UK's trade and the economic slow-down

Total for this question: 50 marks

Study Extracts A, B and C, and then answer all parts of the question that follows.

Extract A

The UK balance of payments on current account, £ billions, 1997–2007

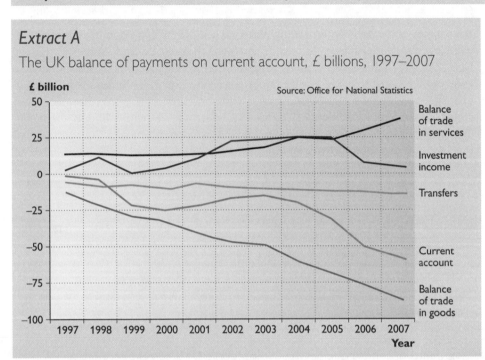

Extract B

The UK starts to wobble

During most of the first decade of the twenty-first century, the pound's exchange rate remained surprisingly high against both the US dollar and the euro. The years of the high value of the pound finally came to an end in August 2008 when sterling's exchange rate fell by more than 8% against the US dollar. The pound also fell against the euro. By September 2008, the pound's trade weighted index had fallen to its lowest level since 1993. Even greater declines followed. 5

Events in the UK and world economies contributed to the pound's fall, and the lower value of the pound in turn is expected to have a significant effect on UK macroeconomic performance. Manufacturing, services and the rate of inflation will all be affected. 10

Adapted from news sources, 2008

Extract C

The UK's macroeconomic performance in 2008

Early in 2008 the UK's rate of economic growth slowed down and the economy teetered on the edge of a recession before falling over the edge. Unemployment grew, as did the rate of inflation for a time, threatening a return to the stagflation of 40 years ago, namely slow or negative growth accompanied by accelerating inflation.

The causes of the UK's deteriorating performance lay partly at home, and partly in   5
world events over which the UK government had little or no control. Domestic causes
were thought to have contributed to deteriorating macroeconomic performance,
as people realised that the earlier boom years had only been kept going through
unsustainable increases in consumer spending and house prices. Overseas causes
included the credit crunch imported from the USA, together with falling US demand   10
for the UK's exports, and growing competition from emerging markets — in particular,
the BRIC countries: Brazil, Russia, India and China.

Adapted from news sources, 2009

[01] **Define the term 'exchange rate' (Extract B, lines 1–2).**   (5 marks)

e It is important to familiarise yourself with the typical layout of the mark scheme for each part of a DRQ. For parts [01] and [05], the mark scheme sets out what is required to earn all 5 of the available marks, but also how an incomplete answer can earn 1, 2, 3 or 4 marks. See the table at the end of the student's answer.

[02] **Identify two significant points of comparison between items in the UK's current account of the balance of payments over the period shown in Extract A.**   (8 marks)

e When answering part [02] or part [05] of a DRQ and quoting statistics to support your points of comparison, you must always state the units in which the data are presented. For this question, the numbers are shown as '£ billion', so make sure that both the '£' sign and the word 'billion' are included against each quoted statistic. For other questions, the units of measurement may take a variety of forms, such as pounds, dollars, kilos and tonnes, and data presented in index number form.

[03] **Explain how a falling exchange rate may affect the current account of the balance of payments.**   (12 marks)

e Part [03] questions test the skill of analysis, which requires you to select relevant information from the data source(s) and then use the information, perhaps as evidence, in the answer. Information in the source is there to prompt your answer. You should indicate which bits of the data you are using, but avoid simply 'copying out' sentences or numbers.

[04]   **Do you agree that the main cause of the UK's deteriorating macroeconomic performance has lain in world events over which the UK government has no control? Justify your answer.**   (25 marks)

e For part [04] and part [08] answers the key skill being tested is evaluation. As this question shows, the word 'evaluate' does not necessarily appear in the question. Other possibilities are 'assess', 'critically discuss' and as in this question 'do you agree?' and 'justify your answer'. Whatever the wording, a 'golden rule' is: 'first analyse, then evaluate'. You must build your evaluation on top of relevant and focused analysis in which economic theory is applied to the issue or issues posed by the question.

A good answer to a part [04] question often shows evaluation alongside the lines of reasoning pursued throughout the answer. You can achieve this by explaining, when you introduce each point or argument, whether it is significant, or whether, though relevant, it is trivial. Your conclusion could then attempt to judge the relative strengths of the arguments discussed in the answer.

Student answers

[01]   The exchange rate is an example of an economic price. **a**

e **2/5 marks awarded.** The mark scheme for a part [01] or [05] question will look something like this:

For an acceptable definition: The price of a currency in terms of another currency The value of a currency expressed as an index number compared to a basket of currencies	**5 marks**
Full marks should be awarded to a student who demonstrates a clear understanding of the term exchange rate even if the definition is not exactly the same as the acceptable examples quoted above.	
Full marks can also be awarded for an accurately labelled exchange rate diagram *provided* the student includes a commentary, relating to the diagram, that shows that she/he understands what is meant by an exchange rate.	
If the definition is incomplete, marks may be broken down, for example, as follows: **a** The exchange rate is an economic price.	**2 marks**

a With this answer, the student fails to provide a sufficiently accurate definition, but nevertheless picks up 2 marks for an incomplete definition.

[02]   A first point of comparison **a** is that the balance of trade in goods is in deficit over the whole 11-year period, whereas the balance of trade in services is in surplus over all the years shown in the data.
For my second point of comparison **a**, of the two 'non-trade' items in the current account, investment income was larger than transfers throughout the data period. The gap between the two was generally widening over the period shown.

e **4/8 marks awarded. a** Although the student makes two sound and significant points of comparison, the points are not backed up with evidence provided by the statistics. The student gains 2 marks for each of the comparative points, but no marks for evidence.

[03] As Extract B states, in August 2008, the pound's exchange rate fell by about 8% against the US dollar, from about $2.00 to the pound to about $1.83 to the pound. This made UK exports to the USA cheaper, and raised the prices for UK residents of imports from America (such as food and computers) and holidays in the USA. Conversely, British goods became cheaper for American residents, as did holidays in the UK.

If Britain's exports and imports reacted in this way to the fall in the exchange rate, the UK's balance of payments on current account would have improved. The huge deficit in 2007 shown in Extract A should have begun to get smaller. However, the deficit may not have shrunk by very much. Two possible reasons are as follows. First, UK goods and services may not be quality competitive (as against the increased price competitiveness won by the falling exchange rate). Second, the UK economy was producing at close to full capacity (and full employment) in the first half of 2008, before the onset of recession. For this reason, the UK may have found it difficult to produce the extra goods to meet increased overseas demand for UK exports.

The circular flow of income also illustrates a possible effect of a falling exchange rate. The resulting fall in imports and increase in exports mean a reduction of leakages of demand (the top horizontal arrow in my diagram below) and an increase in injections into the circular flow (the bottom horizontal arrow). Taken together, there is a net injection of demand into the circular flow which causes real income in the UK to increase. As it increases, demand for imports may increase, and this would offset and possibly eliminate the reduction in the current account deficit initially won by the falling exchange rate.

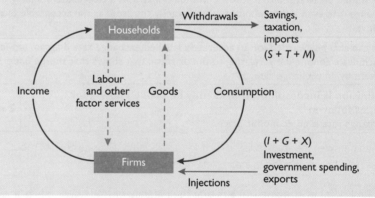

@ **12/12 marks awarded.** This is an excellent answer that would do well at A2 as well as at AS. However, it is over-long for a part [03] answer. The section of the answer that uses circular flow theory to analyse a possible effect of a falling exchange rate could have been left out. Full marks had already been earned by the earlier part of the answer. One point to note is that an ECON 2 DRQ is unlikely to ask students to use a circular flow diagram. This is because the specification only mentions the circular flow of income very briefly and does not indicate that circular flow diagrams *must* be learnt. AD/AS diagrams, by contrast, figure very explicitly in the Unit 2 specification, and questions often require their use in answers. Relevant and accurate application of a circular flow diagram will, of course, by rewarded by the examiner, but it is unlikely to be required in answers.

[04] Extract D states that the causes of Britain's deteriorating macroeconomic performance lay partly at home, and partly in world events over which the UK government had little or no control. If this view is regarded as authoritative, then the question is answered: world events were one of the two causes of Britain's deteriorating economic performance, but a second cause lay in events occurring in the domestic UK economy.

Before developing my answer further, I shall first set out my interpretation of the meaning of 'macroeconomic performance'. The term basically means how well or badly the economy is doing in relation to achieving and maintaining relative full employment, economic growth and higher living standards, control of inflation, and a competitive international trading position. In 2008, the UK's macroeconomic performance could be said to be deteriorating because unemployment was starting to grow, economic growth was slowing down and threatening to become negative (in which case the UK would end up – as it did – in recession), and the rate of inflation was increasing to over 5% (measured by the RPI). But as Extract C indicates, the pound's falling exchange rate was offering a crumb of comfort by increasing the UK's trading competitiveness.

Various international factors certainly contributed to the UK's deteriorating economic competitiveness. These were embodied in the term 'supply shock', the effect of which is illustrated in the following diagram.

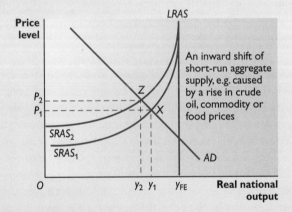

Written on the diagram are three examples of causes of a supply-side shock that in 2008, either separately or in combination, contributed to the UK's deteriorating economic performance. These were rising oil prices, rising commodity prices for goods such as copper, and rising food prices in the early part of the year. By increasing business costs in the UK, all of these contributed to the emergence of cost-push inflation and shifted the UK's *SRAS* curve to the left. In my diagram, output falls (a recession), which means that employment also falls and unemployment rises. A further recent supply-side shock has stemmed from the rising prices of manufactured goods imported from China. For many years the prices of China's exports fell, but now they are rising.

Switching now to events in the UK, it is not true that domestic wage-push inflation has been a significant contributor to the recent deterioration in the

UK's economic performance. This contrasts to the situation 40 years ago which is mentioned in Extract C, when 'stagflation' occurred (economic stagnation accompanied by accelerating inflation). At that time, trade union militancy within the UK, as well as international events such as the first oil crisis, was arguably a major cause of deteriorating economic performance.

However, there have been some other significant domestic factors that contributed in 2008 to the deterioration in macroeconomic performance. Two factors were an overheated housing market and the build-up of household indebtedness. When the house price bubble burst in 2008, it immediately destroyed consumer confidence. Consumers simply stopped spending, which deflated the domestic economy. In this case, the *AD* curve shifted to the left, contracting the levels of output and employment. Likewise, when people, particularly those who had bought their houses at the top of the market with large mortgages, were hit by the rising interest rates brought in to combat the cost-push inflation, they also stopped spending. (Since then very low interest rates have replaced high interest rates, first to prevent the recession getting worse, and second to try to trigger economic recovery.)

Domestic events such as these cannot be completely separated from the international causes of deteriorating economic performance. Extract C mentions the credit crunch imported from the USA. US banks stopped lending to their customers, which reduced demand for UK exports. However, the crunch itself spread to the UK. Following the collapse of the Northern Rock bank, the whole of the UK banking system became reluctant to lend to UK firms and consumers.

@ **22/25 marks awarded.** This is an excellent answer which, despite the lack of a concluding paragraph, reaches Level 5 for the sheer quality of the student's analysis and ongoing evaluation. However, the answer does not really evaluate the extent to which the UK government has control over the international causes of the UK's macroeconomic performance. Among the good points are the way the student attacks the question head-on at the beginning of the answer, and also the explanation of the meaning of macroeconomic performance. (ECON 2 exam questions frequently refer to macroeconomic performance, national economic performance or simply economic performance. All three terms basically mean the same and it is always a good idea to state what the specified term means.) A third good point is the relevant and accurate use of *AD/AS* analysis, together with the accompanying diagram.

Scored 40/50 = good grade A

National income, economic growth and the economic cycle

1 A capital good, such as a machine used by industry, is a physical good used for producing other goods. Human capital is human beings or workers who are hired to produce goods. Investment in education and training improves the quality of human capital.

2 Gross investment is total investment, or spending on capital goods, taking place in an economy. Net investment is the part of total investment that increases the size of the national capital stock (whereas replacement investment makes good the wear and tear that would otherwise reduce the size of the national capital stock).

3 Two diagrams are appropriate. The first is a production possibility diagram showing the outward movement of the economy's *PPF* curve. The second is an *AD/AS* diagram, showing the long-run aggregate supply (*LRAS*) curve shifting to the right.

4 The economic cycle is often called the business cycle, and an old-fashioned name can also be used: the trade cycle.

Aggregate demand and the circular flow of income

5 Consumption occurs when members of households spend their income on consumer goods and services. Saving is income which is not spent on consumption. Investment is spending by firms on capital goods.

6 An increase in the rate of interest causes households to save rather than to consume. Firms often borrow funds to finance investment in new capital goods. An increase in the rate of interest raises the cost of borrowing and reduces investment. When the rate of interest falls, the opposite happens.

7 A budget deficit run by the government is an injection of spending into the circular flow of income. It increases aggregate demand. By contrast, a balance of payments deficit on current account is a leakage or withdrawal of spending from the circular flow. It decreases aggregate demand.

8 The investment multiplier and the accelerator both relate to the relationship between investment and national income, but they work in opposite directions. With the multiplier, a change in investment leads to a change in national income. With the accelerator, a change in national income affects the level of investment.

The aggregate demand and aggregate supply macroeconomic model

9 Students often confuse aggregate demand with national expenditure. Whereas aggregate demand means *planned* spending by households, firms, the government and the overseas sector on real national output, national expenditure (which is the same as national income) measures *actual* spending on output, for example in 2011. Aggregate demand is about what people intend to do in the future; national expenditure is a record of what they end up doing.

10 Macroeconomic equilibrium relates to the aggregate economy, i.e. the economy as a whole, occurring when $AD = AS$ (and when $S + T + M = I + G + X$). By contrast, microeconomic equilibrium, which is a key concept in Unit 1, occurs when supply equals demand in a single market *within* the economy, e.g. the market for apples. Microeconomics disaggregates the economy into the many markets that make up the economy.

11 Inflation is a continuing and persistent rise in the average price level over a period of time. Deflation is the opposite, namely a continuing and persistent fall in the average price level over a period of time. Very often, however, economists use the word deflation to describe a decrease in aggregate demand leading to output falling, or its rate of growth slowing down.

12 Demand-side or Keynesian economists usually focus on how a cut in the rate of income tax increases aggregate demand, shifting the *AD* curve to the right. By contrast, supply-side and pro-free market economists argue that income tax cuts should be used, not to manage aggregate demand, but to create supply-side incentives in the economy. Along with other supply-side policies, income tax cuts can shift the *LRAS* curve to the right.

Policy objectives and conflicts

13 Economic growth is *defined* as an increase in the potential level of output an economy can produce or, in the case of short-run growth, as an increase in output resulting from making use of spare capacity, including labour. Economic growth is *measured* by the percentage annual rate of increase in real GDP.

14 Keynesian macroeconomic policy is interventionist whereas pro-free market macroeconomic policy is anti-interventionist. Keynesian policy assumes that markets perform better when managed by the government; free-market policy assumes the opposite.

15 A policy conflict occurs when it is impossible to achieve two or more policy objectives at the same time. A policy trade-off is an attempt to resolve the conflict by achieving satisfactory, though not perfect, performance with regard to the conflicting objectives.

Employment, unemployment, inflation and deflation

16 The purpose of economic activity is to improve the welfare of all of the population. A necessary condition for improving people's welfare is that everyone who wants to work should be able to work.

17 The literal definition of full employment is no unemployment. However, because the economy is constantly changing, there will always be some frictional, structural and seasonal unemployment.

18 Keynes is most associated with cyclical unemployment, which is also called demand-deficient and Keynesian unemployment.

19 If a government misdiagnoses the main cause of unemployment, then the policy it uses to try to reduce unemployment is likely, at best, to be ineffective and, at worst, to damage the economy, for example by causing inflation.

20 Fifty years ago, wages rising faster than labour productivity were identified as the main cause of cost-push inflation. In recent years, wage rises have not been significant, so increased costs of imported food, raw materials and energy, e.g. oil, are now said to be the main causes of cost-push inflation.

The balance of payments on current account

21 Exports are one of the components of aggregate demand and an increase in exports shifts the AD curve to the right. By contrast, imports are a leakage or withdrawal of spending from the circular flow of income. An increase in imports shifts the AD curve to the left.

22 Although capital flows are an A2 rather than an AS topic, it is useful to know at AS that outward capital flows, which occur when UK firms invest overseas, generate inward investment income in future years (a current account item).

23 A balanced economy is one in which the manufacturing sector and the service sector are both of significant size, without one sector dominating the other to an excessive extent.

Fiscal policy

24 If you refer back to Figure 7 and the accompanying analysis on pages 22–23, you will to see how expansionary fiscal policy increases aggregate demand, causing real national output and the price level to rise. A contractionary fiscal policy would have the opposite effect.

25 In contrast to the answer to knowledge check question 24, supply-side fiscal policy aims to shift the LRAS curve to the right. This is illustrated in panel (c) of Figure 8.

26 Both multipliers measure the relationship between a change in the particular component of aggregate demand (government spending or investment) and the resulting change in nominal national income. If any of the other components of aggregate demand change (consumption or exports), there will be a multiplier effect. A change in taxation or imports can also have a multiplier effect, though in these cases the effect will be negative.

27 In a progressive tax system, the proportion of a person's income paid in tax *increases* as income rises, while in a regressive tax system, the proportion paid in tax *falls* as income increases.

Monetary policy

28 Monetary policy is implemented by the Bank of England (the central bank in the UK), whereas fiscal policy is implemented by the Treasury.

29 Officially, the main monetary policy objective in the UK is the 2.0% inflation rate target set by the Treasury, though in recent months monetary policy has been used mainly to promote recovery from recession. The main monetary policy instrument is Bank Rate which is set monthly by the Monetary Policy Committee at the Bank of England.

30 Each month households with large mortgages pay interest on their mortgages to the bank or building society from which they have borrowed. An increase in mortgage interest rates raises the cost of borrowing, leaving mortgagees with less disposable income to spend on consumption.

31 When interest rates are cut in the UK it becomes less profitable for owners of speculative capital to keep their funds on deposit in UK bank accounts or in UK government bonds. Speculators move their funds into other currencies, which increases the supply of pounds on foreign exchange markets. Excess supply of pounds causes the exchange rate to fall. UK exports become more price competitive and imports become less competitive. Exports increase, imports fall, and the current account improves.

Supply-side policies

32 Demand-side economic policy focuses on managing aggregate demand and shifting the AD curve to the right or to the left. By contrast, the main emphasis of supply-side economic policy is on improving competitiveness and efficiency in the markets that make up the economy. This involves shifting the LRAS curve to the right.

33 Supply-side economists support income tax cuts, not to increase aggregate demand, but to create supply-side incentives for people to work harder, to be entrepreneurial, and to save and invest.

34 One of the main ways of increasing competitiveness and efficiency is to increase labour productivity (output per worker) and capital productivity (output per unit of capital). Indeed, without such productivity increases, it is largely impossible to increase cost competitiveness within the economy.

35 For a supply-side economist, the term 'crowding in' refers to cutting the size of the public sector in order to free resources for the private sector to use. 'Crowding in' is the opposite of 'crowding out', which occurs (according to supply-side economists) when the public sector stifles or displaces private sector activity.

Evaluating national economic performance

36 The Unit 2 specification mentions the performance of the UK economy and macroeconomic performance. ECON 2 DRQs often require you to explain or evaluate the effect of some event, such as an increase in interest rates, on UK macroeconomic performance. The term is therefore a vital one for you to understand. In the context of the ECON 2 exam, national economic performance, the performance of the UK economy and macroeconomic performance can be regarded as interchangeable terms.

37 Surveys of consumer confidence or spending intentions provide a lead indicator of what might happen in the future. Information about spending on imports in the previous year is a lag indicator of what has recently happened in the UK economy.

38 The different phases of the economic cycle are the recovery, the boom, the downturn or recessionary phase, in addition to the peak and trough of the cycle. Note that the downturn only results in a recession if, according to the official UK definition, real output falls for 6 months or more.

39 The acronym BRIC stands for Brazil, Russia, India and China, with the latter being arguably the most important of the four countries for its contribution to world economic growth and trade. The BRIC countries are significant, not only because of the size and growth of their economies, but because they are 'emerging market' countries. In recent years 'emerging market' countries have fast been replacing European Union countries, and possibly the USA, as the engine of global economic growth.